The Trinity

Guided

1   Outline **three** ways the Trinity is reflected in worship by Christians today.

The Trinity is used in the Nicene Creed.

> You are required to give three different ideas to answer this question – do this by putting each idea in its own sentence.

1) One way the trinity is reflected in worship is by making signs of the cross and offer in the name of the Father, Son and Holy Spirit.

2) Another way is prayers such as the Lord's prayer, Nicene creed and Apostles' Creed refer to the Trinity

3) some church hymns refer to the trinity

(3 marks)

Guided

2   Explain **two** reasons why the Trinity is important to Christians.

The Trinity helps Christians to understand the three ways God is revealed. Christians can understand God better by relating to these three aspects: as God the Father, God the Son and God the holy Spirit

> Remember, you need to develop each reason you give in order to answer the question. To do this, you could explain **what** the three ways that God is revealed are for the first reason and **how** the Trinity is a central belief in Christianity for the second.

The Trinity is important because it is the central belief of the Christian religion. If you do not believe in the trinity then you are not seen as a Christian

(4 marks)

D1364446

1

Had a go ☐   **Nearly there** ☐   **Nailed it!** ☐

Interpretations of Creation

1   Outline **three** Christian beliefs about Creation.

> 1) The world was made in 6 periods.
>
> 2) One the first day, beginning, God created creation heaven and the earth was created.
>
> 3) The first day light was created.

> Make sure that the three beliefs you give are different from each other. For example, saying 'some Christians believe the Creation story is a myth' and 'some Christians believe the story is metaphorical' are essentially the same thing and so would only be credited once. Remember, you are not required to explain your answers.

(3 marks)

2   Explain **two** reasons why the Creation account is important to Christians.

> One reason why it is important to Christians is because it helps Christians to understand the purpose of the world. For example, "God created the heaven and earth". From this we could understand that the earth is a test so we could enter heaven.

> Give your first reason why the Creation account is important to Christians (for example, it helps Christians to understand the purpose of the world).

> Next, develop the reason you have given – either by giving an example or including new information to explain the reason more fully.

> Finally, give your second reason (for example, Creation shows the power that Christians believe God has) and develop it in the same way as the first reason.

(4 marks)

The Incarnation

1   Outline **three** Christian beliefs about Jesus as incarnate.

...1)...Jesus!...incarnation...

....

....

....

....

....

....   **(3 marks)**

> You need to identify three different beliefs but you are not required to explain or develop them for this question.

Guided

2   Explain **two** reasons why the Incarnation is important for Christians.

In your answer you must refer to a source of wisdom and authority.

The belief in Jesus as incarnate Son of God is important

as it helps Christians understand what God is like.

....

....

....

....

....

....

....

....

....

....   **(5 marks)**

> Remember that this type of question requires you to give and develop two different reasons. You **must** also refer to a source of wisdom and authority for one of the reasons you explain. This could involve using a direct quote or describing what a Christian source of authority says in your own words. This can appear anywhere within your answer – including at the beginning.

Had a go ☐ Nearly there ☐ Nailed it! ☐

The last days of Jesus' life

In this question, 3 of the marks awarded will be for your spelling, punctuation and grammar, and your use of specialist terminology.

1 "The suffering and death of Jesus is the most important part of his life."

Evaluate this statement considering arguments for and against.

In your response you should:

- refer to Christian teachings
- reach a justified conclusion.

....

....

....

....

....

....

....

....

....

....

....

....

....

....

....

....

....

....

....

....

....

....

....

....

....

....

(15 marks)

> This type of question requires the skill of evaluation. You need to consider the statement carefully and think of reasons to agree and disagree with it. Your reasons must refer to Christian teachings and at the end, after considering all the arguments, you are required to give an overall justified conclusion.

> First, consider arguments that **agree** with the statement. Develop each argument by explaining it fully, and adding examples and Christian teachings – with quotes from sources of authority if possible.

> Next, consider arguments that **disagree** with the statement. Again, make sure they are developed and linked to Christian teachings.

> Lastly, after considering all of the arguments, write a final conclusion. Make sure you provide reasoned judgements based on the evidence you have given in your answer.

> Remember: there are 3 extra marks available in this question for spelling, punctuation and grammar (SPaG), and the use of special terms, so check your answer carefully.

Please complete your answer on your own paper if you need more space.

Salvation

1 Outline **three** Christian beliefs about the importance of atonement and salvation.

....

....

....

....

....

....

....

....   **(3 marks)**

> Atonement and salvation are key ideas for Christians – you need to offer three ideas about why this is. Think about how the relationship between God and humanity is being restored, confirming belief in God and allowing humans to understand the importance of these ideas.

2 Explain **two** ways Christians understand the atonement of Jesus.

....

....

....

....

....

....

....

....

....   **(4 marks)**

> This question requires you to give two different ways in which atonement is understood. Consider how it may show a divine sacrifice, the victory of good over evil or the price being paid for forgiveness.

Life after death

1   Outline **three** Christian beliefs about life after death.

....

- After life people would be judged
by God

....

....

....

....

....

(3 marks)

> Remember that you
> need to give three
> different beliefs. Put
> each one in a different
> sentence.

> **Guided**

2   Explain **two** Christian beliefs about life after death.

Some Christians believe heaven and hell may not be

physical places. ....

....

....

....

Some Christians believe that those who deserve it will go to heaven.

....

....

....

....

....

(4 marks)

> You could include
> interpretations of whether
> heaven and hell are physical
> places or whether Christians
> believe all or only some
> people go to heaven. Make
> sure you develop each
> reason by adding new
> information or examples.

Evil and suffering

1   Outline **three** ways evil and suffering are a problem for Christians.

....

....

....

....

....

.... **(3 marks)**

> **Guided**

2   Explain **two** reasons why evil and suffering may challenge the nature of God for
Christians.

The presence of evil and suffering in the world challenges

the idea of God as all-powerful. ....

....

....

....

....

....

....

.... **(4 marks)**

> Develop this reason by
> adding an example to
> further explain the point
> you have made. **Then** go on
> to give a second reason to
> fully answer the question.
> Make sure you develop
> this second reason by
> adding new information or
> an example to show your
> understanding.

Solutions to evil and suffering

In this question, 3 of the marks awarded will be for your spelling, punctuation and grammar, and your use of specialist terminology.

1   "Evil and suffering prove that God does not exist."

Evaluate this statement considering arguments for and against.

In your response you should:

- refer to Christian teachings
- reach a justified conclusion.

> With an evaluation question like this, it may be useful to plan your answer first and consider what arguments you are going to use. Make sure you develop every argument and reason you include.

....

....

....

....

....

....

....

....

....

....

....

....

....

....

....

....

....

....

....

....

....   **(15 marks)**

Please complete your answer on your own paper if you need more space.

Marriage

> **Guided**

1 Outline **three** Christian beliefs about the purpose of marriage.

Christians believe that one purpose of marriage is to have a sexual relationship.

A second belief is ....

....

....

.... **(3 marks)**

> Give each of your ideas in a separate sentence and make sure that each belief is different.

2 Explain **two** reasons why Christians believe it is important to get married.

....

....

....

....

....

....

....

.... **(4 marks)**

Sexual relationships

1 Outline **three** Christian beliefs about sexual relationships.

....

....

....

....

....

.... **(3 marks)**

Guided

2 Explain **two** reasons why Christians believe sexual relationships should only take place within marriage.

Christians believe casual sex is wrong. ....

> Develop this reason by adding a Christian teaching.

....

....

....

....

> Add a second reason here, making sure you develop it fully by giving new information or an example.

....

.... **(4 marks)**

Families

1 Outline **three** Christian beliefs about family.

....

....

....

....

....

....

(3 marks)

> Make sure you give three different and distinct beliefs held by Christians.

Guided 2 Explain **two** purposes of the family for Christians.

Christians believe the family was God's intention for humans so that a married couple could have children.

....

....

....

Christians believe the family unit provides stability and security.

....

....

....

(4 marks)

> Two purposes of the family for Christians have been identified – you are required to develop them. To do this, add new information, an example or a quote to reinforce the purposes given.

Roles within the family

Guided   **1**   Outline **three** roles parents have in the family.

Parents have a responsibility to keep their children safe.

> Give three different roles – put each one in its own sentence to make them clear.

....

....

....

....

.... **(3 marks)**

2   Explain **two** Christian beliefs about the role of parents in the family.

In your answer you must refer to a source of wisdom and authority.

> Remember that this type of question requires you to give and develop two different reasons. You **must** also include a reference to a source of wisdom and authority (such as the Bible) for one of the reasons you explain.

....

....

....

....

....

....

....

....

....

....

.... **(5 marks)**

The family in the local parish

1 "Counselling provided by the local Church is the best way of supporting families in the local parish."

Evaluate this statement considering arguments for and against.

In your response you should:

- refer to Christian teachings

- reach a justified conclusion.

> Remember that the Church provides many different ways of supporting families in the local community – this includes worshipping together, celebrating rites of passage and parenting classes, as well as counselling. You could choose to include these examples in your answer and argue that some methods may be better than others.

....

....

....

....

....

....

....

....

....

....

....

....

....

....

....

....

....

....

....

....

....

....

....

(12 marks)

Please complete your answer on your own paper if you need more space.

The family in the parish today

1 Outline **three** ways the local parish can support families.

....

....

....

....

....

....

> The local parish helps the family in various ways – through worship, providing classes, rites of passage and counselling, to name a few. Choose three and put each idea in its own full sentence.

(3 marks)

Guided

2 Explain **two** reasons why support given to families from the local parish is important.

Support from the parish allows families to socialise

in their community. This is shown through ....

....

....

....

> Complete each reason given here by developing it. For the first reason, add new information that explains the point being made; for the second one, give a suitable example.

Support given by the parish can offer practical help when families are

struggling. For example, ...

....

....

....

(4 marks)

Family planning

1 "Christians should not use contraception."

Evaluate this statement considering arguments for and against.

In your response you should:

- refer to Christian teachings
- refer to different Christian points of view
- reach a justified conclusion.

> Remember that this question requires you to include Christian teachings – perhaps think about what the Bible teaches. Christians do not all hold the same views. You need to show awareness of this in your answer before you reach a justified conclusion at the end.

....

....

....

....

....

....

....

....

....

....

....

....

....

....

....

....

....

....

....

....

....

.... **(12 marks)**

Please complete your answer on your own paper if you need more space.

Divorce

Guided   1   Explain **two** reasons why some Christians believe divorce is wrong.

Some Christians believe divorce is wrong because

marriage is intended to be for life. ....

....

....

....

....

....

....

....

> Develop the first reason given here by adding further information about where the idea of marriage being for life comes from – think of the marriage vows. Then add a second reason and develop it.

(4 marks)

2   Explain **two** ways Christians may respond to the issue of divorce.

In your answer you must refer to a source of wisdom and authority.

....

....

....

....

....

....

....

....

....

....

....

> Remember that Christians hold different views about divorce – for example, Catholics do not accept it, while Protestants do not like it but will accept it as a last resort. You could choose to reflect these views in your answer.

(5 marks)

Men and women in the family

1   Explain **two** reasons why Christians believe men and women in the family are equal.

In your answer you must refer to a source of wisdom and authority.

....

....

....

....

....

....

....

....

....

....

....

....

....

....

....

> To answer the question, give your first reason and then develop it by adding an example or new information to explain the point you have made.

> Next, give a second reason, making sure it is different from the first. Again, make sure you develop your point by adding new information or an example to explain your understanding.

> You need to add a quote from a source of authority for either one of your two different reasons. Make sure it develops one of the reasons you have given in your answer.

(5 marks)

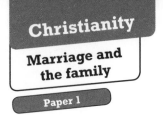
Gender prejudice and discrimination

1   "Gender discrimination is always wrong."

Evaluate this statement considering arguments for and against.

In your response you should:

* refer to Christian teachings
* refer to different Christian points of view
* reach a justified conclusion.

> Remember to include teachings in your answer – for example, refer to what the Bible teaches about this topic. Also show an awareness of why some Christians may hold different views. Conclude your answer by bringing all of your arguments together in a final summary about the statement.

....

....

....

....

....

....

....

....

....

....

....

....

....

....

....

....

....

....

....

....

....

....

.... **(12 marks)**

Please complete your answer on your own paper if you need more space.

Christian worship

Guided

1 Outline **three** ways in which Christians worship.

Christians may take part in the Eucharist.

....

....

....

....

....

....   **(3 marks)**

> Remember that this question requires you to give three different and separate ideas.

2 Explain **two** reasons why some Christians may prefer liturgical forms of worship.

....

....

....

....

....

....

....

....

....   **(4 marks)**

> Liturgical worship is when Christians worship according to a set pattern on a regular basis. Consider why some Christians may prefer this to less formal and unstructured worship. Make sure you give each reason clearly and develop it by giving further information or examples.

The role of sacraments

1   Outline **three** sacraments performed by Christians.

> Give each sacrament in a separate sentence and make sure you have provided three different examples.

....

....

....

....

....

....

....

(3 marks)

> Guided

2   Explain **two** reasons why the Eucharist is important to some Christians.

In your answer you must refer to a source of wisdom and authority.

> You must refer to a source of authority (such as the Bible, Jesus or the 39 Articles) in the explanation for one of your two reasons.

The Eucharist remembers an important historical event for Christians.

....

....

....

....

....

....

....

....

....

(5 marks)

The nature and purpose of prayer

In this question, 3 of the marks awarded will be for your spelling, punctuation and grammar, and your use of specialist terminology.

1 "The Lord's Prayer is the most important prayer for Christians."

Evaluate this statement considering arguments for and against.

In your response you should:

- refer to Christian teachings
- refer to different Christian points of view
- reach a justified conclusion.

> Possible special terms might include: prayer, God, traditional, silently, recited, forgiveness, teachings, Jesus, disciples, worship, denominations, formal, private and personal.

....

....

....

....

....

....

> First, consider arguments that **agree** with the statement. Develop each argument by explaining it fully, and adding examples and Christian teachings – with quotes from sources of authority if possible.

....

....

....

....

> Next, consider arguments that **disagree** with the statement. Again, make sure they are developed and link to Christian teachings.

....

....

....

....

....

> Lastly, after considering all of the arguments, write a final conclusion. Make sure you provide reasoned judgements based on the evidence you have given in your answer.

....

....

....

....

> Remember: there are 3 extra marks available in this question for SPaG and the use of special terms, so check your answer carefully.

....

....

....

(15 marks)

Please complete your answer on your own paper if you need more space.

Pilgrimage

1 Outline **three** activities Christians may do on pilgrimage.

....

....

....

....

....

.... **(3 marks)**

> Remember that you do not need to be specific about an individual place of pilgrimage – think about general things that Christians do while on pilgrimage to any important place.

Guided 2 Explain **two** purposes of pilgrimage for Christians.

Christians believe that going on a pilgrimage will help them

to get closer to God. ....

....

....

....

Christians believe that going on a pilgrimage will help them to better

understand the history and roots of their religion. ....

....

....

.... **(4 marks)**

> Remember that you can include examples such as Jerusalem, Lourdes, Taize and Walsingham as development to show your understanding in your answer to this question.

Celebrations

1 Explain **two** reasons why Christians believe it is important to celebrate Easter.

> Easter is a Christian festival that remembers the death of Jesus and celebrates his resurrection. Consider reasons why this is so important to Christians. Develop each idea that you identify in your answer.

....

....

....

....

....

....

....

....

....   **(4 marks)**

2 Explain **two** ways Christians celebrate Christmas.

> Make sure that you give two different ways and develop each one individually, either by adding new information or giving examples or quotes.

....

....

....

....

....

....

....

....

....   **(4 marks)**

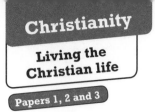

Had a go ☐   Nearly there ☐   Nailed it! ☐

The future of the Church

In this question, 3 of the marks awarded will be for your spelling, punctuation and grammar, and your use of specialist terminology.

1 "All Christians should take part in evangelical work."

Evaluate this statement considering arguments for and against.

In your response you should:

- refer to Christian teachings
- reach a justified conclusion.

> Remember that 'evangelical work' refers to the spreading of faith by missionaries. Think about reasons to agree such as: sharing faith is part of being a Christian; service to others through helping them is considered a positive action; and the Bible contains teachings that support evangelical work. Consider also reasons to disagree such as: faith is a private and personal thing; faith should not be forced onto others; and Christians can help others in a range of ways that does not include evangelical work.

....

....

....

....

....

....

....

....

....

....

....

....

....

....

....

....

....

....

....

> Remember: there are 3 extra marks available in this question for SPaG and the use of special terms, so check your answer carefully.

....

....

....

....

.... **(15 marks)**

Please complete your answer on your own paper if you need more space.

The church in the local community

1   Outline **three** ways the local church community helps people.

....

....

....

....

....

....   **(3 marks)**

> Guided

2   Explain **two** reasons why the local church is important.

The church can help to unite people in the local

community.

....

....

....

| Develop this reason by adding an example, a quote or some new information to further explain the point that has been made. |

....

....

| Now add a second reason – remember to develop it fully. |

....

....

....   **(4 marks)**

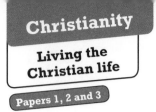
The worldwide Church

In this question, 3 of the marks awarded will be for your spelling, punctuation and grammar, and your use of specialist terminology.

1   "Christians should always help others."

Evaluate this statement considering arguments for and against.

In your response you should:

- refer to Christian teachings
- reach a justified conclusion.

> With an evaluation question like this, it is a good idea to plan your answer first – perhaps by noting down three or four key ideas you wish to use. Make sure you develop every argument and reason you include.

....

....

....

....

....

....

....

....

> Think about Christian teachings that suggest Christians should help others – 'A new command I give you: love one another.' (John 13:34)

....

....

....

....

....

....

> Arguments that disagree with this statement are more challenging – think about why people should help themselves to improve their own lives.

....

....

....

....

....

....   **(15 marks)**

Please complete your answer on your own paper if you need more space.

Origins and value of the universe

> **Guided**

1 Outline **three** Christian beliefs about the origin of the universe.

Christians believe that God is the creator of the universe.

....

....

....

....

....

....

| This answer has started well – the student has given one Christian belief about the origin of the universe. You need to give two further Christian beliefs to be successful in answering this question. |

(3 marks)

> **Guided**

2 Explain **two** reasons why Christians believe the universe is special.

In your answer you must refer to a source of wisdom and authority.

Christians believe the universe was created as a gift

from God. ....

....

....

....

....

| You need to develop this answer by adding further explanation of the reason given – perhaps by referring to the Bible. You also need to link either this reason or the second reason below to a quote from a source of wisdom and authority. |

Christians also believe ....

....

....

....

....

(5 marks)

Sanctity of life

Guided   1   Outline **three** Christian beliefs about the sanctity of life.

Christians believe that God created human life, which makes it sacred.

....

....

....

....

....   **(3 marks)**

2   Explain **two** reasons why belief in the sanctity of life is
important to Christians today.

....

....

....

....

....

....

....

....

....   **(4 marks)**

> Make sure that you give two
> different reasons. Give each
> reason and then develop it by
> adding an example, a quote or
> some new information to fully
> explain each one.

Human origins

1   Explain **two** Christian responses to the scientific theory of evolution.

> Remember that there are two main Christian responses:
>
> 1   to accept both religious and scientific explanations of human origins, **or**
>
> 2   to reject scientific explanations and accept only religious explanations of human origins.
>
> Make sure these are the two responses you include – explaining each one fully.

....

....

....

....

....

....

....

....

.... **(4 marks)**

2   Explain **two** reasons why scientific theories of human origins may cause problems for Christians.

> Think about how evolution challenges the idea that God created humans.

....

....

....

....

....

....

....

.... **(4 marks)**

Christian attitudes to abortion

1 "Christians should never support the use of abortion."

Evaluate this statement considering arguments for and against.

In your response you should:

- refer to Christian teachings

- refer to different Christian points of view

- reach a justified conclusion.

> Abortion is a controversial topic for Christians – they do not always agree. Demonstrate your understanding of this by showing why some Christians may accept abortion in certain circumstances and others will not. Use Christian teachings to support the points you make.

....

....

....

....

....

....

....

....

....

....

....

....

....

....

....

....

....

....

....

....

....

.... **(12 marks)**

Please complete your answer on your own paper if you need more space.

Life after death (1)

Guided 1 Outline **three** Christian beliefs that support the existence of life after death.

Christians believe that Jesus' resurrection proves there is

life after death. ....

....

....

....

....

....

....

> Add two more Christian beliefs that support the view that there is an afterlife. Remember to put each belief in a new sentence.

(3 marks)

Guided 2 Explain **two** reasons why a belief in life after death is significant for Christians.

Christians believe that the afterlife is their ultimate reward

for a life lived as God intended. This belief affects how they

live, behave and act towards others, as they wish to

achieve their eternal reward in heaven with God.

> Make sure that the second reason you give is different from the first and developed by giving an example or new information.

....

....

....

....

....

....

(4 marks)

Life after death (2)

1   "Everyone should believe in life after death."

Evaluate this statement considering arguments for and against.

In your response you should:

- refer to Christian teachings
- refer to non-religious points of view
- reach a justified conclusion.

....

....

....

....

....

....

....

....

....

....

....

....

....

....

....

....

....

....

....

....

....

....

....

....

....   **(12 marks)**

> First, consider arguments that **agree** with the statement. This means including Christian reasons for accepting a belief in life after death. Add teachings to support the points you make.

> Next, consider arguments that **disagree** with the statement. This could include non-religious reasons for not accepting a belief in life after death.

> Lastly, after considering all the arguments, give a final conclusion. Remember that this does not have to be your personal opinion – you can just consider the arguments presented and draw a conclusion from them.

Please complete your answer on your own paper if you need more space.

Euthanasia

> You may use the same content to answer the two questions below – but note that the first is an **outline** question asking you to state three pieces of information, while the second is an **explain** question so you will need to develop the reasons you give in your answer.

Guided

1 Outline **three** reasons why Christians do not accept euthanasia.

Christians believe in the sanctity of life.

It is murder.

It is against the 10 commandment.

(3 marks)

2 Explain **two** reasons why Christians view euthanasia as wrong.

Euthanasia is seen as suicide / murder. This is a major sin in christianity.

Also, Euthenasia ruins someones chance to live. This would prevent them from getting any good deeds.

(4 marks)

Issues in the natural world

1 "Christians have a duty to protect animals."

Evaluate this statement considering arguments for and against.

In your response you should:

- refer to Christian teachings

- refer to different Christian points of view

- reach a justified conclusion.

> With an evaluation question like this, think about jotting down some key ideas or arguments before you start so you know how your answer will progress. Make sure you develop every argument and reason you include.

....

....

....

....

....

....

....

....

....

....

....

....

....

....

....

....

....

....

....

....

....

....

.... **(12 marks)**

Please complete your answer on your own paper if you need more space.

Justice

1 Outline **three** Christian beliefs about justice.

....

....

....

....

....

.... **(3 marks)**

> **Guided**

2 Explain **two** reasons why Christians believe justice is important.

Christians believe God always acts in a just and fair way,

and they should follow his example. ....

....

....

....

| Develop this answer by adding an example, a quote or some new information to the reason already given. |

Christians also believe ....

....

....

| Make sure that your second reason is different from the first and develop it in the same way. |

.... **(4 marks)**

Had a go ☐   Nearly there ☐   Nailed it! ☐

Crime

Guided   **1** Outline **three** actions taken by the Prison Fellowship to end crime.

The Prison Fellowship organises victim awareness

programmes.

> Add two further different ideas, each one in a separate sentence.

....

....

....

....

....

.... **(3 marks)**

2 Explain **two** Christian teachings on crime.

> Give two different teachings, making sure you develop each one fully.

....

....

....

....

....

....

....

.... **(4 marks)**

Good, evil and suffering

1   "There is a reason why people suffer."

Evaluate this statement considering arguments for and against.

In your response you should:

- refer to Christian teachings

- refer to non-religious points of view

- reach a justified conclusion.

> Remember that this question requires you to include Christian views as well as non-religious views. Think about what both believers and non-believers would say about this statement and what evidence they would give to support their views. Try to include a range of reasons in your answer.

....

....

....

....

....

....

....

....

....

....

....

....

....

....

....

....

....

....

....

....

....

....

....   **(12 marks)**

Please complete your answer on your own paper if you need more space.

Had a go ☐   Nearly there ☐   Nailed it! ☐

Punishment

1   Explain **two** reasons why Christians may support the use of punishment.

In your answer you must refer to a source of wisdom and authority.

> Remember to give each reason and then develop it by providing more information or an example.

> Make sure you include a link from one of your reasons to a source of authority or wisdom, such as the Bible.

....

....

....

....

....

....

....

....

....

....

....   **(5 marks)**

Aims of punishment

1 "Reformation is the main aim of punishment."

Evaluate this statement considering arguments for and against.

In your response you should:

- refer to Christian teachings

- reach a justified conclusion.

> Remember that there are four aims of punishment: protection, retribution, deterrence and reformation. You can use some of these in your answer.

....

....

....

....

....

....

....

....

....

....

....

....

....

....

....

....

....

....

....

....

....

(12 marks)

> At the end of your answer, you should have reached a justified conclusion. This means considering all the reasons (agreement and disagreement) you have included in your answer and deciding what you think the overall conclusion should be and why. It does not need to be a personal opinion, but it can be if you wish.

Please complete your answer on your own paper if you need more space.

Forgiveness

1 Outline **three** Christian beliefs about the importance of forgiveness.

> Make sure that you give three different beliefs, each one in a separate sentence.

....

....

....

....

....

....

....

(3 marks)

Guided

2 Explain **two** Christian teachings about forgiveness.

One teaching is that Christians should forgive others as God has forgiven them. This is stated in the Lord's Prayer.

> Think carefully about possible sources of Christian teachings on forgiveness.

....

....

....

....

....

....

(4 marks)

Treatment of criminals

1 Outline **three** Christian beliefs about how criminals should be treated.

....

....

....

....

....

.... **(3 marks)**

2 Explain **two** reasons why Christians believe criminals should be treated with justice.

....

....

....

....

....

....

....

....

.... **(4 marks)**

> Make sure you read the question carefully. It is asking you why justice is important in the treatment of criminals (even though they have done wrong).

41

The death penalty

1 "Christians should support the death penalty."

Evaluate this statement considering arguments for and against.

In your response you should:

- refer to Christian teachings
- refer to different Christian points of view
- reach a justified conclusion.

> Make sure that you present different Christian viewpoints – not all Christians will agree on an issue such as the death penalty. You could use Christian teachings from the Bible to support the arguments you present. Make sure to develop each of your points fully before moving on to the next one.

....

....

....

....

....

....

....

....

....

....

....

....

....

....

....

....

....

....

....

....

....

....

....

....

....

(12 marks)

Please complete your answer on your own paper if you need more space.

Peace

> **Guided**

1 Explain **two** reasons why peace is important to Christians.

Peace is important to Christians because it is a key

teaching from Jesus. ....

....

....

....

....

....

....

....

.... **(4 marks)**

> Develop the first reason by giving an example of a teaching about peace from Jesus. Then add a second reason and develop it by giving new information, a quote or an example.

2 Explain **two** reasons why Christians view Jesus as a peacemaker.

....

....

....

....

....

....

....

....

....

.... **(4 marks)**

> Think about what Jesus taught and what he did – try to relate these things to your ideas about peace.

Had a go ☐   Nearly there ☐   Nailed it! ☐

Peacemaking

Guided

1   Outline **three** ways Christian organisations work to achieve peace.

Christian organisations educate people all around

the world about the importance of peace.

....

....

....

....

....   **(3 marks)**

> Give each of your ideas in a separate sentence and make sure that they are all different.

2   Explain **two** reasons why Christians work to achieve peace in the world today.

....

....

....

....

....

....

....

....

....   **(4 marks)**

> There are many possible reasons you could give to answer this question successfully. To develop each reason you use, and to illustrate your knowledge and understanding, make sure that you link it to key Christian teachings or examples.

Conflict

1 "Violence will never lead to peace in the world."

Evaluate this statement considering arguments for and against.

In your response you should:

- refer to Christian teachings

- refer to non-religious points of view

- reach a justified conclusion.

> It is a good idea to plan the arguments you want to use in your answer, even if they are only one-word memory prompts. Remember to include teachings to support each point you make that agrees or disagrees with the statement.

....

....

....

....

....

....

....

....

....

....

....

....

....

....

....

....

....

....

....

....

....

....

.... **(12 marks)**

Please complete your answer on your own paper if you need more space.

Had a go ☐ Nearly there ☐ Nailed it! ☐

Pacifism

Guided 1 Outline **three** Christian teachings about pacifism.

The Bible teaches that 'you shall not murder.'

Another teaching is ....

....

....

....

....

.... **(3 marks)**

2 Explain **two** reasons why some Christians may be pacifists.

In your answer you must refer to a source of wisdom and authority.

> Give each reason and then develop it by linking it to a Christian teaching or example.

....

....

....

....

....

....

....

....

....

.... **(5 marks)**

The Just War theory

1   "War is always wrong and can never be justified."

Evaluate this statement considering arguments for and against.

In your response you should:

- refer to Christian teachings

- refer to different Christian points of view

- reach a justified conclusion.

> Make sure you meet all the requirements of this question: show awareness of different Christian beliefs about the statement, include Christian teachings in your answer, support each reason you give with evidence and examples, and, at the end, reach a justified conclusion after considering all of the arguments. Remember that all of the required elements – teachings, a range of views and a justified conclusion – are needed to achieve the top levels.

....

....

....

....

....

....

....

....

....

....

....

....

....

....

....

....

....

....

....

....

....

....

....

....

.... **(12 marks)**

Please complete your answer on your own paper if you need more space.

Had a go ☐   Nearly there ☐   Nailed it! ☐

Holy war

1 Outline **three** Christian beliefs about war.

> Give each of your ideas in a separate sentence, making sure that they are all different.

....

....

....

....

....

....

.... **(3 marks)**

Guided   2 Explain **two** Christian teachings about war.

Christians teach ideas of peace, showing that war is wrong.

> Develop the first reason by adding an example of a teaching about peace. Then think of a different Christian teaching about war and develop this idea in the same way.

....

....

....

....

....

....

....

.... **(4 marks)**

Weapons of mass destruction

1   "The use of weapons of mass destruction can never be justified."

Evaluate this statement considering arguments for and against.

In your response you should:

- refer to Christian teachings
- refer to non-religious points of view
- reach a justified conclusion.

....

....

....

....

....

....

....

....

....

....

....

....

....

....

....

....

....

....

....

....

....

....

.... **(12 marks)**

Please complete your answer on your own paper if you need more space.

Issues surrounding conflict

1 Outline **three** ways Christians can work to overcome problems caused by conflict.

....

....

....

....

....

....

....

> Conflict includes war, terrorism and the use of violence. Think about ways Christians can work to reduce this – for example, by donating money, holding prayer vigils or volunteering. Choose three examples and put each one in a separate sentence.

(3 marks)

2 Explain **two** ways Christians may respond to violence being used in the world.

....

....

....

....

....

....

....

....

....

> Make sure you offer two different ways and develop each one by giving new information or an example to show your understanding.

(4 marks)

Revelation

1 Outline **three** examples of revelation in the Bible.

....

....

....

....

....

....

....

> Think of examples of people in the Bible who have received a direct revelation from God.

(3 marks)

> **Guided**

2 Explain **two** ideas about the nature of God that are shown through revelation in the Bible.

In the Bible, God is shown to be omnipotent – all-powerful. This can be seen in the example of Noah. God was able to create a flood to destroy evil in the world, but he was also able to warn and save Noah and his family.

> The 'nature of God' is what God is like – for example, omnipotent, omniscient, benevolent. This answer has provided one idea about what revelation shows that God is like – it has then given a suitable example to develop it. Add a second idea and example to complete this answer.

....

....

....

....

....

(4 marks)

Visions (1)

1 Outline **three** examples of visions for Christians.

....

....

....

....

....

....

....

(3 marks)

> Name a person who has received a vision in Christianity, for example Saul/Paul.

Guided 2 Explain **two** reasons why visions are important to Christians.

Visions help to show Christians the nature of God. ....

....

....

....

Visions are a method that Christians believe God uses to communicate

messages to them. ....

....

....

....

(4 marks)

> Two reasons have been given here – you need to develop each one. To do this, add an example or further new information.

Visions (2)

Guided

1   "Visions are proof of the existence of God."

Evaluate this statement considering arguments for and against.

In your response you should:

- refer to Christian teachings
- refer to non-religious points of view
- reach a justified conclusion.

> Remember the requirements of this question and try to ensure you include all the elements.

Christians may agree with this statement as they believe visions prove

the existence of God. There are many examples in the Bible, the Christian

holy book, such as the visions of Saul/Paul and Joseph. These help to

confirm Christians' faith and enable them to better understand God.

Visions also help to strengthen Christian beliefs

about the nature of God. These include the idea

that God is omnipotent, omniscient and benevolent.

There are examples of visions that show both God's

power and his love for his creation.

> Continue this answer by suggesting reasons why some people – especially the non-religious – may not accept visions as proof of God's existence. Make sure you explain and develop each argument fully.

....

....

....

....

....

....

....

....

....

....

....

> Complete your answer by writing a justified conclusion. A justified conclusion is one based on all of the good reasons, arguments and evidence you presented in your answer.

....

....

....

....

....

....   **(12 marks)**

Please complete your answer on your own paper if you need more space.

Had a go ☐   Nearly there ☐   Nailed it! ☐

Miracles

Guided

1 Outline **three** examples of miracles in the Bible.

An example of a miracle performed in the Bible is Jesus walking

on water.

....

....

....

....

....

.... **(3 marks)**

> Add a second and third example to fully answer this question.

2 Explain **two** reasons why miracles are important to Christians.

In your answer you must refer to a source of wisdom and authority.

....

....

....

....

....

....

....

....

....

....

.... **(5 marks)**

> Remember that you are required to give a supporting source of authority for one of your two reasons.

Religious experiences

Guided

1 Outline **three** Christian beliefs about religious experiences.

Christians believe religious experiences are proof

of God's existence.

....

....

....

....

....

....

(3 marks)

> Remember that there are many possible answers to this sort of question – make sure you add two more distinct and different ideas.

2 Explain **two** reasons why Christians regard religious experiences as a revelation of God.

....

....

....

....

....

....

....

....

....

(4 marks)

> Revelation means the way in which God is revealed or shown to humans. Religious experiences help to show the nature of God as well as helping Christians to develop a closer relationship with him. Try to use these ideas in your answer.

Prayers

1 Explain **two** reasons why prayers being answered may lead to belief in God.

In your answer you must refer to a source of wisdom and authority.

....

....

....

....

....

....

....

....

....

....

....

....

.... **(5 marks)**

> In the first part of your answer, give one reason to answer the question. Develop it by adding new information or an example to show your knowledge. If you can, add a quote from a source of authority (for example, the Bible). If not, make sure that you add one to your second reason.

> Now add a second reason and, again, make sure you develop it. If you did not link your first reason to a quote from a source of authority, you must include one for your second reason.

The design argument

1 Outline **three** Christian beliefs about God revealed by the design argument.

....

....

....

....

....

....

....

> This question is asking you what the design argument shows about God. Think of the characteristics he is believed to have, for example his omnipotence.

(3 marks)

2 Explain **two** Christian responses to non-religious arguments that the design argument does not prove God's existence.

....

....

....

....

....

....

....

....

....

> Make sure that you give the Christian **response** to the non-religious argument, not the argument itself.

(4 marks)

The cosmological argument

Guided

1 "The cosmological argument proves God exists."

Evaluate this statement considering arguments for and against.

In your response you should:

- refer to Christian teachings
- refer to non-religious points of view
- reach a justified conclusion.

....

....

....

....

....

....

....

....

> Start your answer by giving reasons why Christians may agree with the statement: Aquinas' argument offers good evidence; it reveals the nature of God, which confirms that Christian faith, science and religion can work together.

Non-religious people would not agree with the statement. They would argue that science explains how the world was created through the Big Bang, which means that no reference to God is needed. This means that the cosmological argument, which needs a first cause – or God – is wrong. Non-religious people may also challenge the cosmological argument by asking how God was created, as, if everything does have a cause, he cannot just have come into existence by himself. These are important issues to consider in this debate.

> This part of the answer provides arguments that disagree with the statement – this is the non-religious viewpoint.

....

....

....

....

....

....

....

....

> You need to complete the answer by providing a justified conclusion.

(12 marks)

Please complete your answer on your own paper if you need more space.

Religious upbringing

> **Guided**

1 Outline **three** features of a religious upbringing.

One feature is taking children to church on a Sunday.

....

....

....

....

....

Give two more features to
complete this answer.

(3 marks)

2 Explain **two** reasons why a religious upbringing may lead a person
to believe in God.

....

....

....

....

....

....

....

....

....

Make sure you offer two
different reasons and
develop each one by
giving new information or
an example to show your
understanding.

(4 marks)

Human rights

1 "Everyone deserves the same human rights."

Evaluate this statement considering arguments for and against.

In your response you should:

- refer to Christian teachings
- refer to non-religious points of view
- reach a justified conclusion.

> Include Christian teachings to support your arguments: the belief that all humans were created by God in his image; Jesus' teachings about equality, such as the Parable of the Good Samaritan; and the Golden Rule – 'treat others as you would like to be treated'. Also try to include examples of Christians, such as Martin Luther King Jr or Desmond Tutu, who have campaigned for human rights. Remember that non-religious people may also agree with the statement, but for different reasons.

....

....

....

....

....

....

....

....

....

....

....

....

....

....

....

....

....

....

....

....

> Remember that when you provide arguments disagreeing with the statement, you should give examples of people who do not have access to all human rights, such as criminals. Try to develop each argument fully with examples.

.... **(12 marks)**

Please complete your answer on your own paper if you need more space.

Equality

Guided

1 Explain **two** Christian solutions to inequality in the world.

Some Christians, such as Martin Luther King Jr,

feel that they have a duty to work for equality.

....

....

....

....

> Two reasons have been identified – you need to develop each one. Add an explanation about what Martin Luther King Jr did to work for equality and give an example of what charities do to reduce inequality in the world.

Christians may work with charities to reduce inequality. ....

....

....

....   **(4 marks)**

2 Explain **two** Christian teachings about equality.

In your answer you must refer to a source of wisdom and authority.

> Make sure that you link one of your teachings to a quote from a source of wisdom and authority.

....

....

....

....

....

....

....

....

....

....   **(5 marks)**

Had a go ☐   Nearly there ☐   Nailed it! ☐

Religious freedom

Guided   1 Outline **three** benefits for Christians living in a multifaith society.

A multifaith society encourages greater

tolerance of other religions.

> Remember that this question is focused on **multifaith** societies – this means being represented by or including many different faiths. Be careful not to misinterpret this and think this question is about ethnicity.

....

....

....

....

....

....   **(3 marks)**

2 Explain **two** reasons why religious freedom is important to Christians.

> In your development of each reason, you could link one or other of them to a Christian teaching.

....

....

....

....

....

....

....

....   **(4 marks)**

Prejudice and discrimination

1 "All religions have equal value in today's world."

Evaluate this statement considering arguments for and against.

In your response you should:

- refer to Christian teachings
- refer to different Christian points of view
- reach a justified conclusion.

> Remember that although Christianity teaches that all humans are of equal value, not all Christians accept that all **religions** are of equal value. Try to show awareness of this in your answer.

....

....

....

....

....

....

....

....

....

....

....

....

....

....

....

....

....

....

....

....

....

.... **(12 marks)**

Please complete your answer on your own paper if you need more space.

Racial harmony

> **Guided**

1 State **three** benefits for Christians of living in a multi-ethnic society.

A multi-ethnic society can encourage greater understanding between people from different backgrounds.

....

....

....

....

....

....

....

(3 marks)

> Make sure that your reasons focus on the benefits of a **multi-ethnic** society and not a **multifaith** society – these ideas are commonly mixed up. A multi-ethnic society is focused on people of different races being united and recognising all races as equal.

2 Explain **two** ways Christians have worked for racial harmony.

....

....

....

....

....

....

....

....

....

(4 marks)

> Remember that you can use specific examples to answer this question – such as the work of Desmond Tutu – or include information about more general things that Christians have done to work for racial harmony.

Racial discrimination

1   Explain **two** reasons why Christians feel that racial discrimination causes problems in society.

....

....

....

....

....

....

....

....   **(4 marks)**

Guided

2   Explain **two** Christian teachings about racial discrimination being wrong.

In your answer you must refer to a source of wisdom and authority.

Christians follow the teaching 'love your neighbour as yourself' (Mark 12:31) and believe that everyone should be treated fairly. Christians believe that treating people differently because of their race goes against God's teachings.

....

....

....

....

....

....

....

....

....   **(5 marks)**

> Now give a second teaching that shows Christians believe racial discrimination is wrong. Remember – because the first reason has been linked to a source of authority, this part of the question has been answered successfully.

Had a go ☐   **Nearly there** ☐   **Nailed it!** ☐

Social justice

1 "Everyone has a duty to work for social justice."

Evaluate this statement considering arguments for and against.

In your response you should:

- refer to Christian teachings
- refer to relevant ethical arguments
- reach a justified conclusion.

> This question requires you to refer to ethical arguments in your answer – make sure you include a reference to situation ethics.

....

....

....

....

....

....

....

....

....

....

....

....

....

....

....

....

....

....

....

....

....

....

....

.... **(12 marks)**

Please complete your answer on your own paper if you need more space.

Wealth and poverty

Guided

1 Outline **three** ways Christians can help people living in poverty.

Christians can support charities such as Christian Aid.

....

....

....

....

....

.... **(3 marks)**

> Add two more examples of how Christians can help those in poverty. Give each one in a separate sentence.

2 Explain **two** reasons why Christians believe they should help those in poverty.

....

....

....

....

....

....

....

....

.... **(4 marks)**

> Try to consider the reasons why Christians believe they should help others. You could link them to Christian teachings as well as beliefs.

Had a go ☐   **Nearly there** ☐   **Nailed it!** ☐

The Six Beliefs of Islam

Guided

1   Outline **three** features of the Six Beliefs of Sunni Islam.

One feature of the Six Beliefs of Sunni Islam is belief

in one God.

Another feature is belief in angels. ....

....

...Lastly one othe feature Is the holy books........

....

> This answer has identified two of the Six Beliefs. Add a third belief to complete the answer.

(3 marks)

Guided

2   Explain **two** reasons why the Six Beliefs are important to Sunni Muslims.

The Six Beliefs help all Sunni Muslims to better

understand their religion, Islam. For example, Tawhid,.....

.this...is the...beliefe in the...creaers of......

God. This wenter allew Muslins to...

understand thet allah has no partner.

Another reason is that the Six Beliefs show Sunni Muslims how to live

their lives according to Allah's rules. For example, ..the....holy books,.

this Guides us on hew to the a...

Muslim life to get into the life

after death..

> Two reasons have been given in this answer. Develop each one by adding a suitable example from your knowledge of the Six Beliefs.

(4 marks)

The five roots of 'Usul ad-Din in Shi'a Islam

1 Explain **two** reasons why Tawhid is important to Muslims.

They are important to Shi'a Muslims because they write as Muslims. They are the key beliefs all Muslim hold to be true for example, all Shi'a Muslim believe in Allah as the only God

A second reason is that by holding these beliefs, Shi'a Muslims can udderstand

(4 marks)

> There are many possible reasons including: the five roots of 'Usul ad-Din are all based on the central idea of one God; 'Islam' means 'submission to Allah'; Muslims are aware of Allah in all their actions and direct their daily prayers towards him. Use these (or any other ideas you have) to answer this question successfully.

2 Explain **two** of the five roots of 'Usul ad-Din.

....

....

....

....

....

....

....

....

....

(4 marks)

> The five roots are: Tawhid (oneness of Allah), Adl (divine justice), Nubuwwah (prophethood), Imamah (successors to Muhammad) and Mi'ad (Day of Judgement and the Resurrection). Remember that they are only accepted by Shi'a Muslims and are different from the Six Beliefs accepted by Sunni Muslims – be careful not to get them mixed up!

The nature of Allah

Guided

1 Outline **three** Muslim beliefs about the characteristics of Allah.

Muslims believe Allah is transcendent.

....

....

....

....

....

> Add two other Muslim beliefs about Allah, putting each idea in a separate sentence.

(3 marks)

2 Explain **two** ways the characteristics of Allah are described in the Qur'an.

In your answer you must refer to a source of wisdom and authority.

....

....

....

....

....

....

....

....

....

....

....

....

> Remember that you **must** include a reference from a source of wisdom and authority for one of the two ways you explain – this can appear anywhere in your answer.

(5 marks)

Had a go ☐   Nearly there ☐   Nailed it! ☐

Risalah

1 Outline **three** Muslim beliefs about the importance of prophets in Islam.

....

....

....

....

....

.... **(3 marks)**

Guided

2 Explain **two** reasons why Risalah is important in Islam.

Prophets are important in Islam as Allah uses them to

communicate with humanity. For example, Ibrahim carried

messages from Allah to encourage people to worship God.

....

....

....

....

....

....

.... **(4 marks)**

> This answer has given one reason and then developed it using the example of Ibrahim. You need to give a different second reason and then develop it using another example (e.g. Muhammad).

Muslim holy books

> **Guided**

1   Outline **three** features of the Qur'an.

The Qur'an was revealed to Muhammad. ....

....

....

....

....

....

....   **(3 marks)**

> Give two more features of the Qur'an, making sure they are different from the piece of information already given.

2   Explain **two** reasons why the Qur'an is important to Muslims.

....

....

....

....

....

....

....

....

....   **(4 marks)**

> Make sure that you fully develop each reason you give. Give the reason in one sentence and then add a second sentence that either gives new information about the reason or an example.

Malaikah

In this question, 3 of the marks awarded will be for your spelling, punctuation and grammar, and your use of specialist terminology.

1 "Belief in angels is the most important belief in Islam."

Evaluate this statement considering arguments for and against.

In your response you should:

- refer to Muslim teachings
- reach a justified conclusion.

> Remember that Muslims have many key beliefs, including one God (Tawhid), life after death (akhirah) and angels (malaikah). You need to consider a range of arguments about the statement before coming to a justified conclusion.

....

....

....

....

....

....

....

....

....

....

....

....

....

....

....

....

....

....

....

....

....

(15 marks)

> Remember that there are 3 extra marks available in this question for spelling, punctuation and grammar (SPaG) and the use of special terms, so check your answer carefully.

Please complete your answer on your own paper if you need more space.

Had a go ☐   **Nearly there** ☐   **Nailed it!** ☐

Al-Qadr

> **Guided**

1   Outline **three** Muslim beliefs about al-Qadr.

Muslims believe that Allah controls everything. ....

....

....

....

....

....   **(3 marks)**

2   Explain **two** ways in which a belief in al-Qadr affects the lives of Muslims.

....

....

....

....

....

....

....

....

....

....

....

....

....   **(4 marks)**

> Give your first piece of information to answer this question and then develop it by adding new information or an example in a second sentence. Remember that this development must be linked directly to both the information you have given in your first sentence and the question itself.

> Give your second piece of information and develop it in the same way as your first. Remember that this development should add new information about your chosen reason.

Akhirah

1 Outline **three** Muslim beliefs about akhirah.

....

....

....

....

....

....

....

> State three separate ideas held by Muslims about life after death.

(3 marks)

2 Explain **two** ways in which Muslim beliefs about the afterlife are similar to the main religious tradition of Great Britain.

....

....

....

....

....

....

....

....

....

....

> For this question, it may be worth jotting down some brief ideas about the afterlife that you think are similar for both Muslims and Christians. For example: life is seen as a test; ideas of eternal reward and punishment; the concept of resurrection. Then choose two of these ideas to write about in your answer.

(4 marks)

> This style of question can only be asked in this topic (1.8 Beliefs about the afterlife and their significance) and in topic 3.3 (The practice and significance of worship). You will also only be asked to compare and contrast this content in a (b) style exam question.

Marriage

1   Outline **three** Islamic teachings about marriage.

....

....

....

....

....

....

....   **(3 marks)**

> This question is specifically asking what Islam teaches about marriage – make sure your answer focuses on this.

Guided

2   Explain **two** reasons why marriage is significant for Muslims.

Marriage is important to Muslims as it is believed to be

the correct context in which to have a family. Muslims

are expected to get married and to raise their children

within the Islamic faith. ....

....

....

....

....

....

....

....   **(4 marks)**

> You need to give a different second reason to complete this answer. This could be that Allah created men and women for each other to be committed through marriage, that marriage is believed to bring stability to society or that the Qur'an instructs Muslims to marry.

Sexual relationships

> **Guided**

1   Outline **three** teachings about sexual relationships in Islam.

Muslims believe sex is an act of worship.

Islam also teaches ....

....

Another teaching about sexual relationships is ....

....

....   **(3 marks)**

> *Give each teaching in a separate sentence and on a separate line.*

> **Guided**

2   Explain **two** reasons why Muslims believe sex outside marriage is wrong.

In your answer you must refer to a source of wisdom and authority.

Muslims believe that Allah intended sex to take place

only within marriage. ....

....

....

....

....

Muslims also believe ....

....

....

....

....

....   **(5 marks)**

> *Add a sentence to develop this reason and a reference from a source of wisdom and authority (for example, the Qur'an or Hadith) to support it.*

> *Add a second reason here, making sure that you fully develop it by giving new information, a quote or an example. Make sure that it answers the question as well as developing the point you have made.*

Families

Guided

1   "The most important purpose of family for Muslims is to strengthen the ummah."

Evaluate this statement considering arguments for and against.

In your response you should:

• refer to Muslim teachings

• reach a justified conclusion.

Some Muslims agree with the statement as

Muslim families often attend the mosque

together. This helps to unite all Muslims as they

recognise that they are all praying together at

the same time each day. Individual family units

can feel that they have support and are part

of the worldwide ummah through this shared

worship. ....

....

....

....

> Remember that the ummah is the worldwide family of Muslims – the nation. Consider reasons that agree and disagree with the idea that this is the most important purpose of the family in Islam.
>
> Begin your answer by considering why some Muslims may agree with this statement. Make sure that you fully develop each reason you give – you could use Islamic teachings or examples to illustrate the points you make.

A reason to disagree with the statement could

be ....

....

....

....

....

....

....

....

....

....

....

....

....

> Next consider why some Muslims may disagree with the statement – think about what other purposes the family has in Islam in order to come up with reasons.

> Finally, after considering all of your reasons, give a justified conclusion on the statement.

(12 marks)

Please complete your answer on your own paper if you need more space.

The family in the ummah

1   Outline **three** Islamic reasons why it is important for the ummah to provide support to the family.

....

....

....

....

....

....

....

(3 marks)

> This question focuses on **why** the ummah provides support, not what support they provide.

2   Explain **two** ways in which the ummah can support families.

....

....

....

....

....

....

....

....

....

(4 marks)

> Make sure that you give two different reasons and develop each one fully by adding new information or examples.

Had a go ☐   Nearly there ☐   Nailed it! ☐

Contraception

1 "Muslims should not use contraception."

Evaluate this statement considering arguments for and against.

In your response you should:

- refer to Muslim teachings
- refer to different Muslim points of view
- reach a justified conclusion.

> Remember that this question requires you to include Muslim teachings – think about what the different sources of wisdom and authority teach. Muslims do not all hold the same views, so remember to show awareness of this in your answer before you reach a justified conclusion at the end.

....

....

....

....

....

....

....

....

....

....

....

....

....

....

....

....

....

....

....

....

....

....

....

(12 marks)

Please complete your answer on your own paper if you need more space.

Divorce

1 Explain **two** reasons why some Muslims believe divorce is wrong.

....

....

....

....

....

....

....

....

.... **(4 marks)**

> Remember that Muslims believe marriage is important and should be for life as this is what Allah intended. You can use this idea to help you think of two separate reasons.

> Remember that while these two questions seem similar and may refer to similar content, although used differently to answer each question, question 2 requires you to refer to a source of wisdom or authority for one of the two reasons given in your answer.

2 Explain **two** reasons why some Muslims may accept divorce.

In your answer you must refer to a source of wisdom and authority.

....

....

....

....

....

....

....

....

.... **(5 marks)**

Had a go ☐ **Nearly there** ☐ **Nailed it!** ☐

Men and women in the family

1 "Muslim men and women have equal roles in the family."

Evaluate this statement considering arguments for and against.

In your response you should:

- refer to Muslim teachings
- refer to different Muslim points of view
- reach a justified conclusion.

....

....

....

....

....

....

....

....

....

....

....

....

....

....

....

....

....

....

....

....

....

.... **(12 marks)**

Please complete your answer on your own paper if you need more space.

Gender prejudice and discrimination

> **Guided**

1 Outline **three** examples of how Muslims work for gender equality.

Malala Yousafzai stood up against the Taliban to achieve

equality in education. ....

....

> State two more examples of things that Muslims have done to work for equality between men and women.

....

....

....

....   **(3 marks)**

> **Guided**

2 Explain **two** reasons why Muslims believe gender prejudice and discrimination are wrong.

Islam teaches that men and women should be treated the

same way. ....

....

....

....

> Two reasons have been given in this answer. Develop each idea by giving some new information or an example for each one.

Muslims believe that after death Allah will judge men and women in the

same way. ....

....

....

....   **(4 marks)**

Had a go ☐   Nearly there ☐   Nailed it! ☐

The Ten Obligatory Acts of Shi'a Islam

> **Guided**

1 Outline **three** purposes of the Ten Obligatory Acts for Shi'a Muslims.

Shi'a Muslims believe that one purpose is to guide them in how they live their lives.

....

....

....

....

....

....

> Give a total of three separate purposes and make sure that they are all different.

(3 marks)

> **Guided**

2 Explain **two** ways in which Shi'a Muslims practise the Ten Obligatory Acts.

Shi'a Muslims must pray five times a day as one of the

Ten Obligatory Acts. ....

....

....

....

....

> This partial answer has given two ways in which Shi'a Muslims practise the Ten Obligatory Acts – you need to develop each idea by adding an example or new information.

Muslims try to resist temptations that may challenge them in their

daily lives. ....

....

....

....

(4 marks)

The Shahadah

1 Outline **three** reasons why the Shahadah is significant to Muslims.

....

....

....

....

....

.... **(3 marks)**

> **Guided** >

2 Explain **two** ways in which the Shahadah is shown to be important for Muslims today.

The Shahadah is whispered into the ears of newborn

babies. This shows it is important because ....

....

....

....

....

....

.... **(4 marks)**

> To help you answer this question, consider when the Shahadah is spoken: daily; in the ear of a newborn baby; just before death; and recited aloud in front of witnesses.

Had a go ☐   Nearly there ☐   Nailed it! ☐

Salah

In this question, 3 of the marks awarded will be for your spelling, punctuation and grammar, and your use of specialist terminology.

1   "Salah is the most important of the Five Pillars for Muslims."

Evaluate this statement considering arguments for and against.

In your response you should:

- refer to Muslim teachings
- reach a justified conclusion.

....

....

....

....

....

| First, consider arguments that **agree** with the statement, making sure that you develop each one. Think about the regularity of prayer and the fact that it is communication with Allah, which is important to Muslims. |

....

....

....

....

....

....

....

....

....

....

| Next, consider arguments that **disagree** with the statement. Again, make sure they are developed and linked to Muslim teachings. Consider why many Muslims believe Shahadah is more important and, perhaps, the central pillar. |

....

....

....

....

....

| Finally, after considering all of the arguments, give an overall conclusion. Make sure you make reasoned judgements based on the evidence you have given in your answer.

Remember that there are also 3 marks available in this question for SPaG and special terms – so check your answer through carefully. |

....

....

....

....   **(15 marks)**

Please complete your answer on your own paper if you need more space.

Sawm

> **Guided**

1   Outline **three** examples of people who may be excused from fasting during Sawm.

> Give two more examples – each one in a different sentence.

Muslims who are sick may be excused from fasting.

...Women....In....their....periods.:....

...Pregnant....women....are....also....excused.....

(3 marks)

2   Explain **two** reasons why Sawm is important to Muslims.

> Remember to state each reason and then develop it by giving an example, a quote or some new information about the reason. Ensure that your developed reason answers the question and provides more explanation.

...Muslims....become....closer....to....Allah....in....this....

...month.:....By....not....eating....from....Fajr....to....Maghrib....

...you....will....remember....him....and....appreciate....him.:....

(4 marks)

Had a go ☐ **Nearly there** ☐ **Nailed it!** ☐

Zakah and khums

Guided

1 Outline **three** features of Zakah for Muslims.

> These features can include any ideas about Zakah.

Zakah is 2.5 per cent of a Muslim's annual wealth.

....

....

....

....

.... **(3 marks)**

2 Explain **two** reasons why khums is important for Shi'a Muslims.

> Think about each of the following ideas when forming your reasons: khums is used to help the descendants of Muhammad and leaders of the Shi'a faith; it is a duty; it is one of the Ten Obligatory Acts for Shi'a Muslims.

....

....

....

....

....

....

....

.... **(4 marks)**

Hajj

In this question, 3 of the marks awarded will be for your spelling, punctuation and grammar, and your use of specialist terminology.

1   "The benefits of attending Hajj outweigh the challenges."

Evaluate this statement considering arguments for and against.

In your response you should:

- refer to Muslim teachings

- reach a justified conclusion.

> Think about the benefits and challenges of Hajj to help you create arguments that agree and disagree with the statement.

....

....

....

....

....

....

....

....

....

....

....

....

....

....

....

....

....

....

....

....

....

....   **(15 marks)**

Please complete your answer on your own paper if you need more space.

Jihad

1 Outline **three** features of greater jihad.

....

....

....

....

....

....

....

This question is asking you
to give three examples
of the ways a Muslim can
perform greater jihad.
Remember: this is a
personal daily struggle to
be a better Muslim and to
overcome evil.

(3 marks)

> Guided

2 Explain **two** ways in which jihad is understood by Muslims.

Jihad can be interpreted as greater jihad. ....

....

....

....

....

Develop each idea given in
this partial answer.

Jihad can be interpreted as lesser jihad. ....

....

....

....

....

(4 marks)

Celebrations and commemorations

In this question, 3 of the marks awarded will be for your spelling, punctuation and grammar, and your use of specialist terminology.

1   "Celebrating festivals such as Id-ul Adha is vital in Islam."

Evaluate this statement considering arguments for and against.

In your response you should:

- refer to Muslim teachings
- reach a justified conclusion.

> With an evaluation question like this, it is always a good idea to plan your answer first. Consider what arguments might be used to agree and disagree with the statement.

....

....

....

....

....

....

....

....

....

....

....

....

....

....

....

....

....

....

....

....

....   **(15 marks)**

Please complete your answer on your own paper if you need more space.

Origins of the universe

1 Outline **three** Muslims teachings about the origins of the universe.

....

....

....

....

....

....

....

> Write down three **separate** Muslim teachings about how the universe was created.

(3 marks)

> Guided

2 Explain **two** Muslim responses to scientific explanations about the universe.

Some Muslims believe that science and Islam

together explain how the universe was created.

....

....

> One partial response has been given – add a further sentence, example or quote to develop the point that has been made. Then add a second response and develop it in the same way.

....

....

....

....

....

....

(4 marks)

Sanctity of life

1 Outline **three** Muslim teachings about the sanctity of life.

....

....

....

....

....

.... **(3 marks)**

Guided

2 Explain **two** reasons why Muslims believe human life is holy.

Muslims believe human life is holy because it was created by Allah. They believe it should be respected as it was made to be sacred.

> One reason has already been given and developed through explanation. Add and develop a second reason in the same way.

....

....

....

....

....

....

.... **(4 marks)**

The origins of human life

1 "It is possible to accept both evolution and Islamic ideas about the origin of human life."

Evaluate this statement considering arguments for and against.

In your response you should:

- refer to Muslim teachings

- reach a justified conclusion.

> Remember that some Muslims will agree with this statement and others will disagree. You need to show awareness of the reasons for each view in your answer. Think about giving one side of the debate first, then the other, before using the arguments you have included to come to an overall conclusion at the end.

....

....

....

....

....

....

....

....

....

....

....

....

....

....

....

....

....

....

....

....

....

....

(12 marks)

Please complete your answer on your own paper if you need more space.

Muslim attitudes to abortion

1 Explain **two** reasons why some Muslims will not accept abortion.

> Give two different reasons, making sure that you fully develop your explanation of each one by adding new information, a quote or an example.

....

....

....

....

....

....

....

....

....   **(4 marks)**

2 Explain **two** Muslim responses to arguments that abortion is acceptable.

....

....

....

....

....

....

....

....   **(4 marks)**

Death and the afterlife (1)

1　Explain **two** reasons why Muslims support a belief in life after death.

....

....

....

....

....

....

....

.... **(4 marks)**

2　Explain **two** Muslim teachings that support a belief in life after death.

In your answer you must refer to a source of wisdom and authority.

> This question asks specifically for you to focus on Islamic teachings and not generic beliefs.

....

....

....

....

....

....

....

....

.... **(5 marks)**

Death and the afterlife (2)

1   "Everyone should believe in life after death."

Evaluate this statement considering arguments for and against.

In your response you should:

- refer to Muslim teachings
- refer to non-religious points of view
- reach a justified conclusion.

> Make sure that you explain why Muslims believe so strongly in life after death – think of what their sources of authority teach them. Consider also why non-religious people do not generally accept a belief in life after death. You may want to show how Muslims respond to these beliefs in your answer.

....

....

....

....

....

....

....

....

....

....

....

....

....

....

....

....

....

....

....

....

....

....

(12 marks)

Please complete your answer on your own paper if you need more space.

Euthanasia

1 Outline **three** Muslim teachings against euthanasia.

....

....

....

....

....

....

....

(3 marks)

> Read the question carefully – it focuses specifically on **why** Muslims believe euthanasia is wrong.

> **Guided**

2 Explain **two** reasons why Muslims do not accept euthanasia.

In your answer you must refer to a source of wisdom and authority.

Muslims do not accept euthanasia because they believe in the sanctity of life. The Qur'an teaches 'And do not kill yourselves (or one another)' (Surah 4:29). This shows that life is special and sacred as it was created by Allah and, therefore, should not be ended by humans. ....

....

....

....

....

....

....

....

(5 marks)

> One reason has already been given and developed, and includes a quote from a source of authority and wisdom for Muslims. What other quotes could have been used to support this answer? Add a second developed reason to complete the answer.

Issues in the natural world

1 "Muslims should protect animals."

Evaluate this statement considering arguments for and against.

In your response you should:

- refer to Muslim teachings

- refer to different Muslim points of view

- reach a justified conclusion.

> With an evaluation question like this, it is always a good idea to plan your answer first. Make sure that you show why Muslims may hold differing views about this statement.

....

....

....

....

....

....

....

....

....

....

....

....

....

....

....

....

....

....

....

....

....

.... **(12 marks)**

Please complete your answer on your own paper if you need more space.

Had a go ☐   **Nearly there** ☐   **Nailed it!** ☐

Justice

1 "Justice is important for the victims of crime."

Evaluate this statement considering arguments for and against.

In your response you should:

- refer to Muslim teachings

- reach a justified conclusion.

> To answer this question, think about everyone who benefits from justice being achieved – victims, criminals, society in general, etc.

....

....

....

....

....

....

....

....

....

....

....

....

....

....

....

....

....

....

....

....

....

....

....

....

.... **(12 marks)**

Please complete your answer on your own paper if you need more space.

Crime

1   Outline **three** Muslim teachings about crime.

   ....

   ....

   ....

   ....

   ....

   ....   **(3 marks)**

2   Explain **two** ways Muslim organisations work to end crime.

   > Consider the work done by Muslim organisations such as the Muslim Chaplains' Association or Mosaic. Make sure that you specifically focus on what they **do**, giving examples to support your points.

   ....

   ....

   ....

   ....

   ....

   ....

   ....

   ....

   ....   **(4 marks)**

Had a go ☐ **Nearly there** ☐ **Nailed it!** ☐

Good, evil and suffering

1 Outline **three** Muslim teachings about good actions being rewarded.

....

....

....

....

....

.... **(3 marks)**

2 Explain **two** reasons why Muslims believe there is suffering
in the world.

....

....

....

....

....

....

....

....

.... **(4 marks)**

> Make sure that the two reasons
> you give are different. Consider
> including some of the following
> beliefs: suffering is part of
> Allah's plan; suffering is a test
> of faith; some good can come
> from suffering; suffering is
> a reminder of sin; suffering
> is an opportunity to better
> understand the nature of God.

Punishment

> **Guided**

1 Explain **two** reasons why Muslims may view punishment as a form
   of justice.

   In your answer you must refer to a source of wisdom and
   authority.

   > Consider why justice is
   > important to Muslims.

   Muslims believe that justice in the form of fair punishment

   is important when crimes have been committed. This is a

   key idea taught in the Qur'an ....

   ....

   ....

   ....

   > Develop this reason
   > by giving a quote from
   > Surah 2, making sure you
   > explain it in the context of
   > the reason given.

   Muslims also believe that the ummah requires stability

   in society, which can be achieved through just punishment

   when a crime has been committed. ....

   ....

   ....

   ....

   ....

   ....

   > Develop this second
   > reason in the same way as
   > the first.

   (5 marks)

   > You need to link **one** of your reasons to an Islamic source of authority and wisdom.
   > Consider how you could do this for either of the reasons given. Remember that the
   > source can be used anywhere in your answer.

Aims of punishment

1 Outline **three** Qur'anic teachings about punishment.

> Focus on what the Qur'an teaches about punishment – put each teaching in a separate sentence.

....

....

....

....

....

....

....

(3 marks)

2 Explain **two** reasons why the reformation of criminals is important to Muslims.

> Remember that there are many aims of punishment, but you must direct your answer to the reformation of criminals as stated in the question.

....

....

....

....

....

....

....

....

....

....

(4 marks)

Forgiveness

1   "Criminals should always be forgiven."

Evaluate this statement considering arguments for and against.

In your response you should:

*   refer to Muslim teachings

*   reach a justified conclusion.

> Islam teaches about the importance of forgiveness in sources of wisdom and authority such as the Qur'an and Hadith. Think about quoting or paraphrasing ideas from these sources to support your arguments.

....

....

....

....

....

....

....

....

....

....

....

....

....

....

....

....

....

....

....

....

....

....

....

....   **(12 marks)**

Please complete your answer on your own paper if you need more space.

Had a go ☐ **Nearly there** ☐ **Nailed it!** ☐

Treatment of criminals

> **Guided**

1 Outline **three** Muslim attitudes about how criminals should be treated.

Muslims believe criminals should be treated with justice.

....

....

....

....

....

....

....

> Add two more Muslim attitudes about the treatment of criminals to answer this question.

(3 marks)

2 Explain **two** reasons why Muslims believe prisoners' human rights should be protected.

....

....

....

....

....

....

....

....

....

> Think about what human rights prisoners should have – even though they have done wrong. They cannot have full human rights (e.g. their freedom has been removed), but there are reasons why basic human rights, such as the right to food and water, should be upheld.

(4 marks)

The death penalty

1   "Everyone should support the use of the death penalty."

Evaluate this statement considering arguments for and against.

In your response you should:

- refer to Muslim teachings
- refer to non-religious points of view
- reach a justified conclusion.

> Muslims may agree or disagree with this statement, so include both sides of the debate in your answer. Make sure that you also use Islamic teachings to support the arguments you include. Consider what arguments non-religious people might use to support their opinions. Make sure that you include a reasoned conclusion at the end of your answer.

....

....

....

....

....

....

....

....

....

....

....

....

....

....

....

....

....

....

....

....

....

....

....

  (12 marks)

Please complete your answer on your own paper if you need more space.

Peace

1 Outline **three** ways in which Islam is understood as a religion of peace.

....

....

....

....

....

....

....

(3 marks)

> Give three specific examples that show why Islam is a peaceful religion. Think about what 'Islam' means, what the Qur'an teaches and how Muslims demonstrate ideas of peace in their daily lives.

Guided

2 Explain **two** reasons why peace is important to Muslims.

The Qur'an teaches the importance of using 'words of peace' (Surah 25:63). ....

....

....

....

....

All Muslims are part of the ummah, which unites them in *peace*. ....

....

....

....

....

(4 marks)

> Each of these reasons needs development. Add an example, a quote or further information to explain each point.

Peacemaking

1 Explain **two** ways Muslims work for peace.

....

....

....

....

....

....

....

....

....   **(4 marks)**

> Think about the work done by organisations such as Islamic Relief or the Muslim Peace Fellowship as well as how individual Muslims can work for peace.

2 Explain **two** reasons why Muslims believe it is important to work for peace.

....

....

....

....

....

....

....

....

....   **(4 marks)**

> To help you answer this question, you could consider the teachings of Islam, what they teach and why they are important for Muslims.

Conflict

> **Guided**

1 Outline **three** ways Muslims respond to conflict.

Muslims work to bring peace to groups in conflict.

....

....

| Add two more examples of what Muslims do to deal with conflict situations. State each one in its own sentence. |

....

....

....

....   **(3 marks)**

2 Explain **two** Muslim teachings on conflict.

In your answer you must refer to a source of wisdom and authority.

| Remember that **one** of your reasons needs to be linked to a source of wisdom and authority such as the Qur'an. |

....

....

....

....

....

....

....

....

....

....   **(5 marks)**

Pacifism

Guided 1 "Muslims should all be pacifists."

Evaluate this statement considering arguments for and against.

In your response you should:

- refer to Muslim teachings
- refer to different Muslim points of view
- reach a justified conclusion.

Some Muslims may agree with this statement, believing that Islam is a religion of peace and that putting this into practice in the world can best be done through being pacifist. There are many teachings on peace in the Qur'an, showing that violence is not the answer. ....

....

....

....

....

> Continue to develop this section of the answer by giving other reasons in support of the statement.

....

Some Muslims may disagree with this statement as Islam is not traditionally associated with pacifism. ....

....

....

....

> Continue to develop this section of the answer by giving arguments that do not support the statement.

....

....

....

....

....

....

> Bring your answer to a reasoned conclusion – consider all of the reasons you have presented.

....

....

....

....

.... **(12 marks)**

Please complete your answer on your own paper if you need more space.

The Just War theory

1   Outline **three** Muslim conditions of Just War theory.

....

....

....

....

....

....

....   **(3 marks)**

> The Just War theory covers the criteria and conditions that must be met in order to make acceptable and to justify the decision to go to war. You are required to give three examples of these.

2   Explain **two** ways Muslims respond to Just War theory.

....

....

....

....

....

....

....

....

....

....   **(4 marks)**

> Remember that Muslims may respond differently to the Just War theory. Some will support it and recognise it as an option of last resort, while others may reject it altogether. Shi'a Muslims attach importance to this theory as it is one of the Ten Obligatory Acts, whereas Sunni Muslims view it as having less significance.

Holy war

Guided

1   Outline **three** Muslim teachings about war.

The Qur'an suggests that violence can be used if necessary.

> Add two more Islamic teachings about war.

....

....

....

....

....   **(3 marks)**

2   Explain **two** reasons why some Muslims accept holy war.

....

....

....

....

....

....

....

....   **(4 marks)**

Had a go ☐   Nearly there ☐   Nailed it! ☐

Weapons of mass destruction

1 "Weapons of mass destruction should never be used."

Evaluate this statement considering arguments for and against.

In your response you should:

- refer to Muslim teachings
- refer to relevant ethical theories
- reach a justified conclusion.

> Remember to ensure you include all aspects required by this question. This includes Muslim teachings and reference to ethical theories such as utilitarianism.

....

....

....

....

....

....

....

....

....

....

....

....

....

....

....

....

....

....

....

....

....

.... **(12 marks)**

Please complete your answer on your own paper if you need more space.

Issues surrounding conflict

1 Outline **three** ways Muslims work to reduce conflict.

The Muslim Council of Britain runs education programmes.

....

....

....

....

....

.... **(3 marks)**

> Give two more examples of how Muslims or Muslim groups can work for peace in the world.

2 Explain **two** ways Muslims respond to conflict.

....

....

....

....

....

....

....

....

.... **(4 marks)**

> You could include one response where Muslims work to reduce conflict – giving specific examples – and one where they may support the use of conflict.

Revelation

Guided   **1** Outline **three** Muslim beliefs about the Qur'an as a form of revelation of Allah.

> Muslims believe that revelation through the Qur'an shows
>
> them what Allah is like. ....

....

....

....

....

(3 marks)

> Think about how Muslims believe revelation happens, what their main source of revelation is, or perhaps what revelation may reveal about Allah.

2 Outline **three** ideas about the nature of Allah shown through revelation in the Qur'an.

....

....

....

....

....

....

....

(3 marks)

> Think about three characteristics of Allah that are shown to Muslims through revelation in the Qur'an.

Visions

Guided

1   Explain **two** reasons why visions prove the existence of Allah.

Visions show Muslims that Allah is all-powerful

and are proof that he exists. ....

....

....

....

....

....

....

....

> Develop the first reason given here – perhaps by adding an example or further explanation of how the power of Allah is shown. Then add a second reason and develop it in the same way.

(4 marks)

2   Explain **two** reasons why Muslims believe visions do not prove Allah exists.

....

....

....

....

....

....

....

....

....

> Remember that not all Muslims place importance on visions. Identify two reasons why this is and develop each one fully.

(4 marks)

Miracles

1 "Miracles are evidence of Allah's existence."

Evaluate this statement considering arguments for and against.

In your response you should:

- refer to Muslim teachings
- refer to non-religious points of view
- reach a justified conclusion.

> Remember that some Muslims place great importance on miracles, while others do not – you need to show awareness of this in your answer. You might also consider including the Muslim response to non-religious views.

....

....

....

....

....

....

....

....

....

....

....

....

....

....

....

....

....

....

....

....

....

....

.... **(12 marks)**

Please complete your answer on your own paper if you need more space.

Religious experiences

1   Outline **three** Muslim beliefs about the nature of religious experiences.

....

....

....

....

....

....   **(3 marks)**

Guided

2   Explain **two** reasons why religious experiences are important to Muslims.

Religious experiences reveal the nature of Allah.

Muslims believe that Allah's power is shown by

revealing himself to prophets such as Muhammad.

....

> The first part of this answer gives a reason and then successfully develops it, giving more information. To complete this answer, add a second reason and develop it in the same way.

....

....

....

....

....

....

....

....

....   **(4 marks)**

The design argument

1 Outline **three** characteristics of Allah revealed by the design argument.

....

....

....

....

....

....   **(3 marks)**

2 Explain **two** ways in which Muslims may respond to the idea that the design argument does not prove the existence of Allah.

> Make sure that you give two different ways and develop each idea fully.

....

....

....

....

....

....

....

....   **(4 marks)**

The cosmological argument

1 Explain **two** characteristics revealed about the nature of
Allah through the cosmological argument.

> A characteristic is what Muslims believe Allah is like. You need to identify two of these and link them to how the cosmological argument demonstrates that this is what Allah is like.

....

....

....

....

....

....

....

....

....   **(4 marks)**

2 Explain **two** reasons why the cosmological argument is proof that Allah exists.

....

....

....

....

....

....

....

....   **(4 marks)**

The existence of suffering

1 Outline **three** problems the existence of suffering may raise about Allah for Muslims.

> Think about the characteristics of Allah that are challenged by the existence of evil and suffering.

....

....

....

....

....

....

....

(3 marks)

> **Guided**

2 Explain **two** reasons why suffering may cause people to question their belief in Allah.

Suffering may make people question their belief in

Allah as they may ask why Allah doesn't use his

power to prevent suffering. ....

> Develop this reason by adding an example, a quote or some new information. You then need to give a second reason and develop it in the same way.

....

....

....

....

....

(4 marks)

Solutions to the problem of suffering

Guided 1 Explain **two** practical ways in which Muslims respond to the existence of suffering.

Some Muslims may respond by helping out with a charity

that tries to relieve people's suffering. ....

....

....

....

....

Another response could be for Muslims to pray for those who are

suffering. ....

....

....

....

.... **(4 marks)**

> Develop each point given by adding an example, a quote or some new information to fully explain each idea.

2 Explain **two** Muslim teachings about coping with suffering.

In your answer you must refer to a source of wisdom and authority.

> Make sure that you provide a quote for one of the two teachings you include.

....

....

....

....

....

....

....

....

....

.... **(5 marks)**

Human rights

1 "Muslims should always support human rights."

Evaluate this statement considering arguments for and against.

In your response you should:

- refer to Muslim teachings
- refer to different Muslim points of view
- reach a justified conclusion.

....

....

....

....

....

....

....

....

....

....

....

....

....

....

....

....

....

....

....

....

....

....

....   **(12 marks)**

> Start your answer by considering reasons why Muslims may **agree** with the statement. Make sure that you develop every point you make.

> Next, consider why some Muslims may **disagree** with the statement. Give specific examples to support the reasons you offer.

> Finally, after considering all the reasons you have given, present a reasoned conclusion.

Please complete your answer on your own paper if you need more space.

Equality

Guided

1 Outline **three** Muslim practices that show equality.

One example is Muslims all praying at the same time.

....

....

....

....

....

....   **(3 marks)**

> Think of ways in which Muslims try to achieve equality in their religious practices.

2 Explain **two** reasons why Muslims work for equality.

....

....

....

....

....

....

....

....

....

....   **(4 marks)**

> This question focuses on why Muslims work for equality – use examples or teachings to support the points you include.

Religious freedom

1 "Religious freedom is important in a multi-faith society."

Evaluate this statement considering arguments for and against.

In your response you should:

- refer to Muslim teachings

- refer to non-religious points of view

- reach a justified conclusion.

> Make sure you plan which arguments you want to include in your answer. Develop each argument fully, giving evidence or examples to support each one. Review the arguments you included to help you come to a reasoned conclusion at the end of your answer.

....

....

....

....

....

....

....

....

....

....

....

....

....

....

....

....

....

....

....

....

....

....

....

.... **(12 marks)**

Please complete your answer on your own paper if you need more space.

Prejudice and discrimination

1   Explain **two** reasons why Muslims believe prejudice and discrimination are wrong.

In your answer you must refer to a source of wisdom and authority.

....

....

> Give your first reason (for example, because it is a key teaching in the Qur'an).

....

....

....

> Develop your reason by explaining the idea more fully – add new information or an example.

....

....

....

> Give your second reason.

....

....

....

> Develop your second reason in the same way as the first one, by adding an example, a quote or some new information.

....

....

....

> Add a quote from a source of wisdom and authority, for example the Qur'an, to **one** of your two reasons. This can be included anywhere in your answer.

....

....

....

....

....   **(5 marks)**

Racial harmony

Guided

1 Outline **three** Muslim teachings about racial harmony.

Muhammad taught that all mankind is descended from Adam and Eve.

....

....

....

....

.... **(3 marks)**

2 Explain **two** reasons why racial harmony is important to Muslims.

....

....

Make sure that you give two different reasons and develop each idea fully.

....

....

....

....

....

....

.... **(4 marks)**

Racial discrimination

1   Outline **three** Muslim teachings about racial discrimination.

> Give three teachings from Islam about why it is wrong to treat people from different races differently.

....

....

....

....

....

....

.... **(3 marks)**

2   Explain **two** reasons Muslims believe racial discrimination is not acceptable.

> Make sure that you give two different reasons and develop each one fully.

....

....

....

....

....

....

....

.... **(4 marks)**

Had a go ☐ Nearly there ☐ Nailed it! ☐

Social justice

Guided 1 Outline **three** reasons why Muslims work for social justice.

Muslims believe that the Qur'an teaches them to help each other. ....

....

....

....

....

.... **(3 marks)**

Guided 2 Explain **two** Muslim teachings about social justice.

Islam teaches that Muslims will be judged by Allah after

death on the way they helped others. ....

> Make sure that you develop each of the reasons given.

....

....

....

....

The Qur'an teaches that all humans are equal as they are all Allah's

creation. ....

....

....

....

.... **(4 marks)**

Wealth and poverty

1 "All Muslims should share their wealth with others."

Evaluate this statement considering arguments for and against.

In your response you should:

- refer to Muslim teachings
- refer to different Muslim points of view
- reach a justified conclusion.

> Think about planning your answer before you write it. Remember to refer to quotes, examples and evidence to support the reasons you give.

....

....

....

....

....

....

....

....

....

....

....

....

....

....

....

....

....

....

....

....

....

....

(12 marks)

Please complete your answer on your own paper if you need more space.

(a) type questions

Please use your own paper to answer these questions.

(a) type questions are worth 3 marks and ask you to outline or state three things.
These may be beliefs, teachings, features, responses or something else.

> Remember that to be successful in this type of question, you need to simply give three
> correct and accurate pieces of information – you are not required to develop or explain them.

1   Outline **three** of the Six Beliefs of Islam for Sunni Muslims.   **(3 marks)**

2   Outline **three** Muslim beliefs about the Qur'an.   **(3 marks)**

3   Outline **three** ways belief in al-Qadr affects the lives of Muslims.   **(3 marks)**

4   Outline **three** Muslim teachings about sexual relationships.   **(3 marks)**

5   Outline **three** Muslim beliefs about divorce.   **(3 marks)**

6   Outline **three** ways the Shahadah is spoken by Muslims today.   **(3 marks)**

7   Outline **three** features of khums.   **(3 marks)**

8   Outline **three** ways Muslims celebrate Id-ul Fitr.   **(3 marks)**

9   Outline **three** Muslim teachings about why human life is holy.   **(3 marks)**

10 Outline **three** ways Muslims can carry out the role of khalifah.   **(3 marks)**

11 Outline **three** Muslim beliefs about justice.   **(3 marks)**

12 Outline **three** Muslim teachings about punishment.   **(3 marks)**

13 Outline **three** ways Muslims can work for peace.   **(3 marks)**

14 Outline **three** Muslim beliefs about visions.   **(3 marks)**

15 Outline **three** ways Muslims may respond to suffering.   **(3 marks)**

16 Outline **three** Muslim teachings about racial harmony.   **(3 marks)**

(b) type questions

Please use your own paper to answer these questions.

(b) type questions are worth 4 marks and require you to describe or explain two key areas within the Islamic faith. This could include beliefs, teachings, ideas, features, events or ways, to name a few.

> To be successful in this type of question, state two points and then develop each one. This development could be done by adding a second sentence that explains the point you have made, or by adding new information or offering an example. You can also include a relevant quote.

1 Explain **two** of the five roots of 'Usul ad-Din in Shi'a Islam. **(4 marks)**

2 Explain **two** Muslim beliefs about the roles of prophets. **(4 marks)**

3 Describe **two** ways in which beliefs about the afterlife are different for Muslims and Christians. **(4 marks)**

> You must be able to contrast the areas of belief and practice for the topics of the afterlife and worship. This means being able to describe and explain similarities and differences for these topics.

4 Explain **two** reasons why Muslims believe in life after death. **(4 marks)**

5 Explain **two** teachings about the purpose of family in Islam. **(4 marks)**

6 Explain **two** ways the ummah supports the family. **(4 marks)**

7 Explain **two** Muslim teachings about gender prejudice and discrimination. **(4 marks)**

8 Explain **two** purposes of the Ten Obligatory Acts for Shi'a Muslims. **(4 marks)**

9 Explain **two** conditions for declaration of lesser jihad in Islam. **(4 marks)**

10 Explain **two** Muslim beliefs about the origins of the universe. **(4 marks)**

11 Explain **two** Muslim teachings about euthanasia. **(4 marks)**

12 Explain **two** Muslim teachings about forgiveness. **(4 marks)**

13 Explain **two** Muslim beliefs about the use of weapons of mass destruction. **(4 marks)**

14 Explain **two** ways Muslims may respond to challenges to the cosmological argument. **(4 marks)**

15 Explain **two** ways Muslims respond to inequality in the world. **(4 marks)**

(c) type questions

Please use your own paper to answer these questions.

(c) type questions are worth 5 marks and require you to explain key areas within the Islamic faith. This could include beliefs, teachings, ideas, features, events or ways of worship. You also need to add a relevant source of authority for one of the two points given in your answer.

> To be successful when answering this type of question, state two points and then develop each one by adding further new information, an example or a quote. Link in a teaching from a source of wisdom – you are allowed to paraphrase this and it can be part of the point you have made to answer the question.

1   Explain **two** characteristics of Allah shown in the Qur'an.

    In your answer you must refer to a source of wisdom and authority.   **(5 marks)**

2   Explain **two** Muslim teachings about marriage.

    In your answer you must refer to a source of wisdom and authority.   **(5 marks)**

3   Explain **two** different ways Muslims view the roles of men and women in the family.

    In your answer you must refer to a source of wisdom and authority.   **(5 marks)**

4   Explain **two** reasons why Hajj is important for Muslims.

    In your answer you must refer to a source of wisdom and authority.   **(5 marks)**

5   Explain **two** Muslim responses to animals being used for experimentation.

    In your answer you must refer to a source of wisdom and authority.   **(5 marks)**

6   Explain **two** Muslim teachings about the treatment of criminals.

    In your answer you must refer to a source of wisdom and authority.   **(5 marks)**

7   Explain **two** Muslim teachings about war.

    In your answer you must refer to a source of wisdom and authority.   **(5 marks)**

8   Explain **two** ways Muslims may respond to the importance of religious experience.

    In your answer you must refer to a source of wisdom and authority.   **(5 marks)**

9   Explain **two** Muslim teachings about religious freedom.

    In your answer you must refer to a source of wisdom and authority.   **(5 marks)**

(d) type questions

Please use your own paper to answer these questions.

(d) type questions are worth 12 marks and require you to evaluate a stimulus and consider different viewpoints about the significance of a particular aspect of belief.

> There are many requirements of this type of exam question – read the bullet points carefully. Try to give justified reasons that include examples and teachings. You need to use chains of logical reasoning for your arguments – join up your ideas and evidence to reach an overall justified conclusion that is supported by the points you have made.

1 "All Muslims should get married."

   Evaluate this statement considering arguments for and against.

   In your response you should:

   • refer to Muslim teachings

   • refer to non-religious points of view

   • reach a justified conclusion.   **(12 marks)**

2 "Greater jihad is more important than lesser jihad."

   Evaluate this statement considering arguments for and against.

   In your response you should:

   • refer to Muslim teachings

   • refer to different Muslim points of view

   • reach a justified conclusion.   **(15 marks)**

3 "It is never right to fight."

   Evaluate this statement considering arguments for and against.

   In your response you should:

   • refer to Muslim teachings

   • refer to non-religious points of view

   • reach a justified conclusion.   **(12 marks)**

4 "It is wrong for Muslims to be wealthy."

   Evaluate this statement considering arguments for and against.

   In your response you should:

   • refer to Muslim teachings

   • reach a justified conclusion.   **(12 marks)**

> On the exam papers, questions 1 and 3 (the units 'Muslim beliefs' and 'Living the Muslim life') have 3 extra marks available for your use of spelling, punctuation and grammar (SPaG), as well as your use of specialist terminology.

Answers

Christianity

UNIT 1: CHRISTIAN BELIEFS

1 The Trinity

1 One mark will be awarded for each point identified up to a maximum of three marks. (3)
  • The Trinity is used in the Nicene Creed (1).
  • The Trinity is spoken in Sunday services (1).
  • The Trinity is reflected in the words of hymns that are sung (1).
  • The Trinity is a part of how Christians bless themselves (1).
  • The Trinity is part of a Christian baptism service (1).
  Other valid answers will be accepted.
2 One mark will be awarded for providing each reason and a second mark for development of the reason up to a maximum of four marks. (4)
  • The Trinity helps Christians to understand the three ways God is revealed (1). It helps Christians to understand God better through the three ideas of the Father, Son and Holy Spirit (1).
  • The Trinity is important because it is the central belief of the Christian religion (1). Christians accept that all other beliefs (for example, the afterlife) are linked to essential ideas contained in the Trinity (1).
  • The Trinity is mentioned and has an important role in Christian worship (1). For example, it is part of the Nicene Creed and prayers are offered 'in the name of the Father, and of the Son and of the Holy Spirit' (1).
  Other valid answers will be accepted.

2 Interpretations of Creation

1 One mark will be awarded for each point identified up to a maximum of three marks. (3)
  • God created the world (1).
  • Christians may interpret the story literally (1).
  • Genesis in the Bible contains a description of how God created the world (1).
  • The Bible says the world was created in six days (1).
  • The world was created through the Word of God (1).
  Other valid answers will be accepted.
2 One mark will be awarded for providing each reason and a second mark for development of the reason up to a maximum of four marks. (4)
  • The Creation account states that God created the world (1). This shows the power that Christians believe God has (1).
  • It explains how the world came to exist (1). The Bible explains that God created the world for humans to live in (1).
  • It helps Christians to understand the purpose of the world (1). Some Christians accept that science explains how the world came into existence, but the Bible explains why God created the world (1).
  Other valid answers will be accepted.

3 The Incarnation

1 One mark will be awarded for each point identified up to a maximum of three marks. (3)
  • Jesus is the Son of God (1).
  • Jesus is one part of the Trinity (1).
  • Jesus is God in human form (1).
  • Jesus was both human and divine (1).
  • Jesus lived and died within the world (1).
  Other valid answers will be accepted.
2 One mark will be awarded for each reason and a second mark for development of the reason up to a maximum of four marks. One further mark will be awarded for any relevant source of wisdom and authority. (5)

  • The belief in Jesus as incarnate Son of God is important as it helps Christians understand what God is like (1). They can more easily relate to the idea of Jesus as a human than to God as a divine being (1). The Bible explains how God, through Jesus, became flesh and lived among humans, teaching and healing, making it easier for humans to relate to him (1).
  • Christians believe Jesus showed them how to act and behave (1). They feel that Jesus revealed the expectations for humans that God intended they should follow (1). Jesus showed people how to pray (Matthew 6:5–6), in order that they should develop a relationship with God (1).
  • Jesus reflects the characteristics that Christians claim God has (1). God was willing to send his son to Earth to die for the sins of the world, which shows his benevolence (1): 'For God so loved the world that he gave his one and only Son, that whoever believes in him shall not perish but have eternal life.' (John 3:16) (1)
  Other valid answers will be accepted.

4 The last days of Jesus' life

1 "The suffering and death of Jesus is the most important part of his life." Be sure to make your points specific, and refer to teachings and views, as you are instructed. You can support your arguments with biblical or other teachings. Make sure you give balanced views and then draw a conclusion – make sure you say why this is your conclusion. In this question, 3 of the marks awarded will be for your spelling, punctuation and grammar, and your use of specialist terminology. (15)
  Arguments for the statement:
  • Jesus was sent to Earth by God to die for the sins of the whole world and to redeem humanity. This was his purpose and its fulfilment helped to restore the relationship between God and humanity. Christians were shown that by following Jesus' example God could forgive them too.
  • Christian teachings in the Bible reflect the importance of Jesus' suffering and dying. This is still remembered today through the celebration of the Eucharist. Jesus' blood is represented by the wine and his body by the bread in this important service.
  • The suffering and death of Jesus provide hope for all Christians in its confirmation of life after death. Jesus' death and later resurrection show what all Christians hope to achieve in the afterlife – that they can be reunited eternally with God.
  Arguments against the statement:
  • The whole of Jesus' life is important to Christians. Without his birth and events during his life, his death and suffering could not have happened. His entire life gives Christians an example to follow in how to live their lives as God wants.
  • Jesus' resurrection is more important than his suffering and death. God's most important message to humanity is that there is an eternal afterlife, not that Jesus died in order for them to achieve this.
  • Key events in Jesus' life known as 'The Passion' provide the complete message of the example of the life of Jesus. His suffering and death are an important part of this, but perhaps more important is the message that Jesus is God Incarnate and is both human and divine. This is part of the central belief of the Trinity from which all other Christian beliefs stem.
  Other valid answers will be accepted.

5 Salvation

1 One mark will be awarded for each point identified up to a maximum of three marks. (3)
  • Atonement and salvation are believed to restore the relationship between God and humanity (1).

- They confirm belief in an all-loving and powerful God (1).
- They allow humans to understand the importance of being reconciled with other humans (1).
- They confirm belief in life after death (1).
- They give humans hope of reward in the afterlife (1).

Other valid answers will be accepted.

2 One mark will be awarded for providing each way and a second mark for development of the way up to a maximum of four marks. (4)
- Jesus' death is a divine sacrifice (1). It is believed to show God's love for humanity through his willingness to sacrifice the life of his son Jesus (1).
- Atonement shows Jesus' death as good overcoming evil (1). Jesus was used as a ransom to stop the devil having a hold over humanity (1).
- Jesus' death represents the importance of forgiveness (1). It allows humans to move on and have a fulfilling relationship with God where forgiveness has been shown (1).

Other valid answers will be accepted.

6 Life after death

1 One mark will be awarded for each point identified up to a maximum of three marks. (3)
- There is an afterlife for those who believe in God (1).
- Christians believe death is not the end (1).
- The resurrection of Jesus proves there is life after death (1).
- Christians believe in heaven and hell (1).
- Christians believe God will judge humans after death (1).

Other valid answers will be accepted.

2 One mark will be awarded for providing each belief and a second mark for development of the belief up to a maximum of four marks. (4)
- Some Christians believe heaven and hell may not be physical places (1). As the soul is believed to be spiritual rather than physical, this may make more sense (1).
- Some Christians believe that those who deserve it will go to heaven (1). Even if some people do not have faith, if they have lived good lives, they can be rewarded (1).
- Some Christians believe that there will be a Second Coming of Jesus (1). They believe that he is needed to once more save humanity from the sins of the whole world (1).

Other valid answers will be accepted.

7 Evil and suffering

1 One mark will be awarded for each point identified up to a maximum of three marks. (3)
- Evil and suffering can challenge Christians' belief in God's existence (1).
- Christians may question why God does not help those who suffer (1).
- Christians may question the purpose of evil and suffering (1).
- Christians may question why God allows people to commit evil acts (1).
- Christians may question whether God is all-knowing (1).

Other valid answers will be accepted.

2 One mark will be awarded for providing each reason and a second mark for development of the reason up to a maximum of four marks. (4)
- The presence of evil and suffering in the world challenges the idea of God as all-powerful (1). If he was all-powerful and could do anything he would be able to stop evil in the world, therefore perhaps he doesn't exist (1).
- Evil and suffering may lead Christians to question God's benevolence (1). If he was all-loving and cared for his creation he would want to stop evils such as abuse and natural disasters, therefore perhaps he doesn't exist (1).
- Evil and suffering may lead Christians to question God's omniscience (1). If he was all-knowing he would know of human suffering and do something to prevent it, therefore perhaps he doesn't exist (1).

Other valid answers will be accepted.

8 Solutions to evil and suffering

1 "Evil and suffering prove that God does not exist." Be sure to make your points specific, and refer to teachings and views, as you are instructed. You can support your arguments with biblical or other teachings. Make sure you give balanced views and then draw a conclusion – make sure you say why this is your conclusion. In this question, 3 of the marks awarded will be for your spelling, punctuation and grammar, and your use of specialist terminology. (15)

Arguments for the statement:
- The existence of evil and suffering in the world may cause some Christians to question the nature and existence of God, as it appears to contradict what they believe. They may struggle with the challenge this poses and it may affect the strength of their faith.
- The existence of natural evil and suffering is for many the best argument and evidence that God does not exist. There does not seem to be a good explanation for natural suffering in the world, which may offer proof that God does not exist.
- The excessive suffering of some people, including the suffering of innocent people, may lead some Christians to doubt the existence of God; it seems like good evidence to suggest he does not exist.

Arguments against the statement:
- Some Christians may believe that evil and suffering are part of God's plan. They may look to the example of Job in the Bible to argue that evil and suffering have a purpose that humans are not aware of, meaning it is still possible to believe in God.
- Some Christians may believe that God gave humans free will and this at least explains the existence of moral evil. It shouldn't stop Christians believing in God, as humans are seen to be responsible for some of the evils in the world.
- Some Christians may argue that God does not test people more than they can handle and the experience of evil and suffering can make people stronger. As a result of their own experiences, people may spend more time in prayer or charity work, helping others who are suffering.

Other valid answers will be accepted.

UNIT 2: MARRIAGE AND THE FAMILY

9 Marriage

1 One mark will be awarded for each point identified up to a maximum of three marks. (3)
- Christians believe that one purpose of marriage is to have a sexual relationship (1).
- It provides companionship between husband and wife (1).
- It requires that individuals make a lifelong commitment to a person (1).
- It brings stability to society (1).
- It allows people to support each other in a stable relationship (1).

Other valid answers will be accepted.

2 One mark will be awarded for providing each reason and a second mark for development of the reason up to a maximum of four marks. (4)
- After marriage, a couple can have a sexual relationship (1). This is seen as the correct place in which to have a sexual relationship and raise a family (1).
- Some Christians believe that marriage is a sacrament made before God (1). They believe that God is involved in the marriage and blesses the relationship (1).
- Christians believe that marriage forms a stable family unit on which society is built (1). It provides stability for the raising of children in a moral way and gives structure to society (1).

Other valid answers will be accepted.

10 Sexual relationships

1. One mark will be awarded for each point identified up to a maximum of three marks. (3)
   - Sexual relationships should only take place within marriage (1).
   - They should happen between one man and one woman who are married to each other (1).
   - The purpose of a sexual relationship within marriage is to procreate (1).
   - A sexual relationship is a way for a married couple to show their commitment to each other (1).
   - All forms of sexual activity outside marriage are forbidden (1).

   Other valid answers will be accepted.

2. One mark will be awarded for providing each reason and a second mark for development of the reason up to a maximum of four marks. (4)
   - Christians believe casual sex is wrong (1). The Bible teaches that sexual relationships are a gift from God and are special, therefore they should not be abused (1).
   - Christians believe that God intends sex to occur within marriage for the purpose of procreation (1). Marriage provides stability for the couple, their children and for society, and is what God wants for humans (1).
   - The Ten Commandments, which are rules from God, forbid adultery (1). This means that married couples should remain faithful to each other and stay true to their marriage vows (1).

   Other valid answers will be accepted.

11 Families

1. One mark will be awarded for each point identified up to a maximum of three marks. (3)
   - Christians believe that having a family was God's intention for humans (1).
   - Christians believe that the family provides stability for society (1).
   - Christians believe that the family is where children are raised in the Christian faith (1).
   - Christians believe that the family is where children are taught the difference between right and wrong (1).
   - Christians believe that family should follow once a couple is married (1).

   Other valid answers will be accepted.

2. One mark will be awarded for providing each purpose and a second mark for development of the purpose up to a maximum of four marks. (4)
   - Christians believe the family was God's intention for humans so that a married couple could have children (1). It provides the best environment for parents to raise their children as Christians (1).
   - Christians believe the family unit provides stability and security (1). Children can be brought up safely in a loving environment and helped to understand the world (1).
   - Christians believe the family unit is a place where children can be taught (1). Parents have a responsibility to teach their children the difference between right and wrong (1).

   Other valid answers will be accepted.

12 Roles within the family

1. One mark will be awarded for each point identified up to a maximum of three marks. (3)
   - Parents have a responsibility to keep their children safe (1).
   - Parents should raise their children as Christians (1).
   - Parents should love their children (1).
   - Parents should teach their children the difference between right and wrong (1).
   - Parents should attend church with their children (1).

   Other valid answers will be accepted.

2. One mark will be awarded for each belief and a second mark for development of the belief up to a maximum of four marks. One further mark will be awarded for any relevant source of wisdom and authority. (5)
   - Christians believe God's intention for humans when he created them was for married couples to become parents (1). The Bible Creation story includes God's instruction to Adam and Eve to continue the human race (1): 'God blessed them and said to them, "Be fruitful and increase in number; fill the earth and subdue it".' (Genesis 1:28) (1)
   - Parents have a responsibility to raise their children as Christians (1). The Bible teaches that children should learn about Christianity, which also allows the religion to continue to grow (1): 'bring them up in the training and instruction of the Lord.' (Ephesians 6:4) (1)
   - Christians believe they have a duty to care for their children (1). The Bible teaches that parents should provide safety, support and guidance for their children as they are a gift from God (1): 'Children are a heritage from the Lord, offspring a reward from Him.' (Psalm 127:3) (1)

   Other valid answers will be accepted.

13 The family in the local parish

1. "Counselling provided by the local Church is the best way of supporting families in the local parish." Be sure to make your points specific, and refer to teachings and views, as you are instructed. You can support your arguments with biblical or other teachings. Make sure you give balanced views and then draw a conclusion – make sure you say why this is your conclusion. (12)

   Arguments for the statement:
   - Counselling provided by the local Church can be a very important and effective way for a family to discuss their problems and also possible solutions. Counselling sessions can offer the family unit time to listen to each other and respond in a calm environment, which might otherwise not be possible.
   - The Church might be able to offer specially trained Christian counsellors to help families or couples experiencing conflict or difficulties. As members of the Christian community, these counsellors will also ensure that any advice given considers Christian teachings.
   - Church ministers or vicars may also offer individual couples counselling. Advice from someone they know and trust within their local Christian community can have a particularly positive impact – perhaps more so than other more general events the Church might organise to help and support families.

   Arguments against the statement:
   - Although counselling may be seen to have a positive impact, other methods of supporting families in the local parish may be considered to be of more practical use. Worshipping together and spending time together may help families to find things in common and to work together.
   - Some Christians may not feel comfortable with a local parish counsellor or Church minister. They may believe that any problems they face as a family need to be worked out in private and not shared with those outside the family unit.
   - Some Christians may prefer to pray and worship together in order to ask for help in solving their problems. They may believe that teaching children about the faith, celebrating Christian rites of passage and reading Christian teachings are more useful in helping them to work together as a family.

   Other valid answers will be accepted.

14 The family in the parish today

1. One mark will be awarded for each point identified up to a maximum of three marks. (3)
   - The local parish can bring families together through worship (1).

- The local parish can help families celebrate rites of passage together (1).
- The local parish can put on parenting classes (1).
- The local parish can offer counselling to families in difficulties (1).
- The local parish can organise social events to bring people together (1).

Other valid answers will be accepted.

2 One mark will be awarded for providing each reason and a second mark for development of the reason up to a maximum of four marks. (4)
- Support from the parish allows families to socialise in their community (1). This is shown through the marking of rites of passage, such as marriages, which bring the community together (1).
- Support given by the parish can offer practical help when families are struggling (1). For example, counselling can provide moral support, enabling families to work through their problems (1).
- Support for families from the local parish can also strengthen the Church (1). Allowing Christians to come together to share their faith gives them a sense of identity and of belonging to their community (1).

Other valid answers will be accepted.

15 Family planning

1 "Christians should not use contraception." Be sure to make your points specific, and refer to teachings and views, as you are instructed. You can support your arguments with biblical or other teachings. Make sure you give balanced views and then draw a conclusion – make sure you say why this is your conclusion. (12)

Arguments for the statement:
- Catholic Christians believe that every sexual act should be open to the possibility of a child. Using contraception prevents the creation of new life and so goes against what they believe is God's will.
- God gave humans a commandment to have children. The Bible instructs them: 'As for you, be fruitful and increase in number; multiply on the Earth and increase upon it.' (Genesis 9:7) If Christians believe procreation is the purpose of a sexual relationship, a couple using contraception could be seen as defying God.
- Some Christians believe that the use of contraception can encourage casual sex, which in turn could lead to the spread of disease. This goes against what God wants and intended for humans.

Arguments against the statement:
- Some Protestants may believe that contraception is a sensible method of family planning. They accept that God did give humans the commandment to have children, but argue that these children should all be wanted with parents who can provide for them.
- Some Christians argue that there may be situations where the use of contraception is sensible – for example, if the mother's health is at risk or any potential children conceived could be severely disabled.
- Some Christians believe that while artificial methods of contraception may be wrong, natural methods (such as the rhythm method) are not. They may believe that as procreation is still possible, these are more acceptable than artificial methods.

Other valid answers will be accepted.

16 Divorce

1 One mark will be awarded for providing each reason and a second mark for development of the reason up to a maximum of four marks. (4)
- Some Christians believe divorce is wrong because marriage is intended to be for life (1). In the marriage vows, the couple say the words 'till death us do part' (Vows) (1).
- Divorce may be seen as wrong because marriage is a sacrament between the couple and God (1). Marriage is special, sacred and a gift from God, so the promises made before him should not be broken (1).
- Jesus taught that divorce was wrong (1): 'anyone who divorces his wife, except for sexual immorality, and marries another woman commits adultery.' (Matthew 19:9)

Other valid answers will be accepted.

2 One mark will be awarded for each way and a second mark for development of the way up to a maximum of four marks. One further mark will be awarded for any relevant source of wisdom and authority. (5)
- Some Christians do not accept divorce as they believe it goes against what God wants (1). Marriage is intended to be for life, as stated in the words of the marriage vows (1): 'till death us do part' (Vows) (1)
- Christians believe marriage is for life as this is what God intended for humans (1). This key belief is stated in the Bible, therefore they do not recognise divorce (1): 'Therefore what God has joined together, let no one separate.' (Mark 10:9) (1)
- Some Christians do not like divorce but accept that sometimes it may be necessary, as in cases of adultery (1). They recognise that sometimes mistakes are made and some relationships should be allowed to end (1): 'I tell you that anyone who divorces his wife, except for sexual immorality, and marries another woman commits adultery.' (Matthew 19:9) (1)

Other valid answers will be accepted.

17 Men and women in the family

1 One mark will be awarded for each reason and a second mark for development of the reason up to a maximum of four marks. One further mark will be awarded for any relevant source of wisdom and authority. (5)
- The Bible says that God made both man and woman in his image (1). Some Christians believe that this means they were made to be equal (1): 'So God created mankind in his own image, in the image of God he created them; male and female he created them.' (Genesis 1:27) (1)
- Christians believe in the key teaching of equality (1). This is reinforced in the Bible in the teachings of St Paul (1): 'There is neither Jew nor Gentile, neither slave nor free, nor is there male and female, for you are all one in Christ Jesus.' (Galatians 3:28) (1)
- Some Christians believe that men and women were created equal but given different roles (1). Men are seen as the providers, while women are seen as the home-keepers (1): 'It is not good for the man to be alone. I will make a helper suitable for him.' (Genesis 2:18) (1)

Other valid answers will be accepted.

18 Gender prejudice and discrimination

1 "Gender discrimination is always wrong." Be sure to make your points specific, and refer to teachings and views, as you are instructed. You can support your arguments with biblical or other teachings. Make sure you give balanced views and then draw a conclusion – make sure you say why this is your conclusion. (12)

Arguments for the statement:
- Christians believe that God created men and women to be equal. There is a Bible teaching stating that God made both man and woman in his image, showing that they are equally special.
- Some Christian denominations allow both men and women to hold the same authority roles within the Christian Church. Both men and women can become bishops and take responsibility within the structure of the Church.
- Many Christian organisations work against gender discrimination. Organisations such as Tearfund and Christian Aid work for human rights – this includes teaching people

that gender discrimination is wrong. These organisations use Christian teachings such as stewardship and caring for all humans to demonstrate that all people are equal.

Arguments against the statement:

- Some Churches have practices that seem to show gender discrimination still exists. In Catholicism, women are not allowed to hold traditionally male positions such as that of priest, bishop or pope, as these roles represent Jesus, who was male.
- There are Bible teachings that could be interpreted to suggest men and women are not equal. Eve was made from Adam's rib as a 'helper', which could suggest that women are inferior.
- Some Christians believe that although men and women are equal, there are some jobs and roles which may be better suited to one gender or the other. For example, there may be some roles where male or female characteristics are more suitable.

Other valid answers will be accepted.

UNIT 3: LIVING THE CHRISTIAN LIFE

19 Christian worship

1 One mark will be awarded for each point identified up to a maximum of three marks. (3)
- Christians may take part in the Eucharist/Holy Communion/Mass (1).
- Christians may dance or clap during worship (1).
- Christians may spend time in personal/private prayer (1).
- Christians may worship in silence (1).
- Christians may worship through singing (1).
Other valid answers will be accepted.

2 One mark will be awarded for providing each reason and a second mark for development of the reason up to a maximum of four marks. (4)
- Christians may feel that liturgical forms of worship offer a set structure and pattern which is easier to follow (1) – for example, having set hymns and prayers means they know what to expect (1).
- They may feel that it brings them closer to God (1). The Church gives instructions for how Christians should worship – following these instructions means Christians can better connect with God because they are doing what he wants (1).
- Some Christians may feel that certain important religious rituals are performed only as part of liturgical worship (1), for example the Eucharist/Holy Communion/Mass. This service re-enacts the Last Supper with the bread and wine representing the body and blood of Jesus Christ (1).
Other valid answers will be accepted.

20 The role of sacraments

1 One mark will be awarded for each point identified up to a maximum of three marks. (3)
- One sacrament is infant baptism (1).
- One sacrament is adult baptism (1).
- One sacrament is confirmation (1).
- One sacrament is the Eucharist/Holy Communion/Mass (1).
- One sacrament is marriage (1).
Other valid answers will be accepted.

2 One mark will be awarded for each reason and a second mark for development of the reason up to a maximum of four marks. One further mark will be awarded for any relevant source of wisdom and authority. (5)
- The Eucharist remembers an important historical event for Christians (1). This event is the Last Supper, which was the last meal that Jesus shared with his disciples (1): 'The Lord Jesus, on the night he was betrayed, took bread, and when he had given thanks, he broke it and said, "This is my body,

which is for you; do this in remembrance of me." In the same way, after supper he took the cup, saying "This cup is the new covenant in my blood; do this, whenever you drink it, in remembrance of me".' (1 Corinthians 11:23–25) (1)
- Some Christians believe the bread and wine used in the ceremony represent the sacrifice Jesus made (1). The bread represents the body of Jesus while the wine represents the blood (1): 'This is my body given for you. ... This cup is the new covenant in my blood, which is poured out for you.' (Luke 22:19–20) (1)
- The Eucharist helps Christians understand their faith better and allows them to get closer to God (1). Celebrating the Eucharist is a way for believers to share their faith through Jesus (1): 'Sacraments ordained of Christ be not only badges or tokens ..., but rather they be ... effectual signs of grace, and God's good will towards us, ... which ... confirm our Faith in him.' (39 Articles XXV) (1)
Other valid answers will be accepted.

21 The nature and purpose of prayer

1 "The Lord's Prayer is the most important prayer for Christians." Be sure to make your points specific, and refer to teachings and views, as you are instructed. You can support your arguments with biblical or other teachings. Make sure you give balanced views and then draw a conclusion – make sure you say why this is your conclusion. In this question, 3 of the marks awarded will be for your spelling, punctuation and grammar, and your use of specialist terminology. (15)
Arguments for the statement:
- The Lord's Prayer is the most common Christian prayer. It is taught to children when they are young, used as part of many Christian services and recited by Christians in times of need, thus demonstrating its importance within Christianity.
- The Lord's Prayer contains key essential Christian teachings. It talks about God and who he is, as well as asking for forgiveness from God for the things people have done wrong. These beliefs are crucial to being a Christian.
- The Lord's Prayer is believed to have been taught to the disciples by Jesus, thus demonstrating its importance. Prayer is a way of communicating with God and thanking him or praising him for what he has done. The Lord's Prayer is a set prayer used by many Christians to do this.
Arguments against the statement:
- Although prayer is important to all Christians, different people may prefer different styles of prayer. For example, some denominations may prefer to sing or dance as part of their worship of God and therefore would not place as much importance on a set prayer such as the Lord's Prayer.
- Some Christians worship in different ways in order to connect with God. Quakers, for example, sit in silence and only speak when needed, so they may place less importance on formal set prayers.
- Although the Lord's Prayer is important because it was taught by Jesus to his followers, some Christians may prefer personal or private prayer where they can speak directly to God from their own hearts. This may not include set prayers such as the Lord's Prayer – these people may feel that more informal prayer helps them to connect with God on a deeper level.
Other valid answers will be accepted.

22 Pilgrimage

1 One mark will be awarded for each point identified up to a maximum of three marks. (3)
- Christians may spend time reflecting on the importance of the place of pilgrimage (1).
- Christians may pray for forgiveness (1).
- Christians may spend time in a Christian order (1).
- Christians may visit a shrine or place of importance (1).
- Christians may spend time in meditation (1).
Other valid answers will be accepted.

2 One mark will be awarded for providing each purpose and a second mark for development of the purpose up to a maximum of four marks. (4)

- Christians believe that going on a pilgrimage will help them to get closer to God (1). They feel they will understand their faith better (1).
- Christians believe that going on a pilgrimage will help them to better understand the history and roots of their religion (1). For example, Christians go to Jerusalem to see where Jesus died (1).
- Christians believe that going on a pilgrimage will allow them to take time out of their lives in order to focus and concentrate on their religion (1). It will help them to consider the important teachings and beliefs they hold to be true (1).

Other valid answers will be accepted.

23 Celebrations

1 One mark will be awarded for providing each reason and a second mark for development of the reason up to a maximum of four marks. (4)

- Easter is the festival that remembers the crucifixion and celebrates the resurrection of Jesus (1). This event is central to the Christian faith and proves that Jesus was the Son of God (1).
- The event of the resurrection of Jesus helps Christians to have faith in eternal life after death (1). It confirms their belief in the promise God has made to them of a reward after death if they have followed the example of Jesus (1).
- The events remembered during the festival of Easter help to strengthen Christians' beliefs about the characteristics of God (1). It confirms their belief in Jesus as part of the Trinity and his nature as both human and divine (1).

Other valid answers will be accepted.

2 One mark will be awarded for providing each way and a second mark for development of the way up to a maximum of four marks. (4)

- Christians may attend Midnight Mass on Christmas Eve (1). This service celebrates the birth of Jesus (1).
- Christian children may put on nativity plays (1). These commemorate the events that led up to the birth of Jesus (1).
- Christians may attend a special service on Christmas Day (1). They may sing carols and share in the celebrations with other Christians (1).

Other valid answers will be accepted.

24 The future of the Church

1 "All Christians should take part in evangelical work." Be sure to make your points specific, and refer to teachings and views, as you are instructed. You can support your arguments with biblical or other teachings. Make sure you give balanced views and then draw a conclusion – make sure you say why this is your conclusion. In this question, 3 of the marks awarded will be for your spelling, punctuation and grammar, and your use of specialist terminology. (15)

Arguments for the statement:

- Taking part in evangelical work helps to secure the future of the Church and allows it to grow. Evangelism helps to ensure the continued growth of the religion. It may also be the only way some people gain knowledge of faith.
- Some Christians feel they have a duty from God to share their faith with others. The New Testament teaches: 'Go into all the world and preach the gospel to all creation.' (Mark 16:15)
- There is a long history of missionary and evangelical work in Christianity. By taking part in this, Christians can help to continue the work of prominent missionaries such as William Carey and Eric Liddell.

Arguments against the statement:

- Some Christians may feel that faith is a personal thing that should be kept private, and that it is not necessary to share faith with other people.

- The fact that there has been a tradition of taking part in evangelical work does not mean it should always be this way. With society changing, it may no longer be appropriate to be preaching and sharing faith.
- Some Christians place more importance on evangelical work than others. Not all denominations agree that they should be sharing their faith. Some may believe they have other duties – such as charity work and helping others – that don't involve sharing their faith and beliefs.

Other valid answers will be accepted.

25 The church in the local community

1 One mark will be awarded for each point identified up to a maximum of three marks. (3)

- The local church may hold clubs for children (1).
- The local church organises social events such as coffee mornings (1).
- The local church brings Christians from different denominations together (1).
- The local church works with families to resolve issues (1).
- Christians from the local community may visit those in hospital (1).

Other valid answers will be accepted.

2 One mark will be awarded for providing each reason and a second mark for development of the reason up to a maximum of four marks. (4)

- The church can help to unite people in the local community (1). It finds things that bring them together, for example by organising community activities (1).
- The church provides practical support and help (1), such as resources for families in need (1).
- The church community can give advice (1). Vicars or elderly couples in the community can help people who are experiencing difficulties and need advice or help (1).

Other valid answers will be accepted.

26 The worldwide Church

1 "Christians should always help others." Be sure to make your points specific, and refer to teachings and views, as you are instructed. You can support your arguments with biblical or other teachings. Make sure you give balanced views and then draw a conclusion – make sure you say why this is your conclusion. In this question, 3 of the marks awarded will be for your spelling, punctuation and grammar, and your use of specialist terminology. (15)

Arguments for the statement:

- Christians believe they are all part of the worldwide Church and therefore have a duty to help and care for other people in society. Many Bible teachings support this idea, for example: 'A new commandment I give you: love one another. As I have loved you, so you must love one another.' (John 13:34)
- Christians believe they need to follow the example of Jesus, who taught about helping others. The Bible Parable of the Good Samaritan teaches that helping others is putting Christian teachings into action.
- Charities such as Christian Aid have been set up to help others. Its aim is to eradicate poverty and improve life for all people in the world as it believes this is a God-given responsibility.

Arguments against the statement:

- Christians may want to help other people in society, but question whether the help of one person can make a significant difference. Many Christians believe that only those people with power and authority can make change happen.
- There are examples of Christians who have dedicated their lives to helping others. While it is good to follow their example, some have been killed doing so, which shows this approach can sometimes be dangerous.

- Some people may feel that they do not have a responsibility to help those outside their own circle of family and friends, especially if they are not religious. Although they may accept that religious believers such as Christians feel they have a duty to do so, many people feel this is not their responsibility.
Other valid answers will be accepted.

UNIT 4: MATTERS OF LIFE AND DEATH

27 Origins and value of the universe

1 One mark will be awarded for each point identified up to a maximum of three marks. (3)
- Christians believe that God is the creator of the universe (1).
- Christians believe that the world was created as a gift from God for humanity (1).
- Some Christians believe that the creation of the world took six days (1).
- Some Christians believe that the seventh day of Creation was a day of rest for God (1).
- Some Christians believe that God caused the 'Big Bang' that started the universe (1).
Other valid answers will be accepted.
2 One mark will be awarded for each reason and a second mark for development of the reason up to a maximum of four marks. One further mark will be awarded for any relevant source of wisdom and authority. (5)
- Christians believe the universe was created as a gift from God (1). God set apart the seventh day of creation as a holy day intended for people to use as a day of rest and worship (1): 'Then God blessed the seventh day and made it holy, because on it he rested from all the work of creating that he had done.' (Genesis 2:3) (1)
- Christians believe humans were given stewardship over the universe (1). This is a God-given responsibility to care for the world, thus showing how important it is (1): 'The Lord God took the man and put him in the garden of Eden to work it and take care of it.' (Genesis 2:15) (1)
- Christians believe that God planned the universe carefully with humans in mind (1). The Bible teaches that the creation of the world and humanity did not happen by chance (1): 'Then God said, "Let us make mankind in our image, in our likeness".' (Genesis 1:26) (1)
Other valid answers will be accepted.

28 Sanctity of life

1 One mark will be awarded for each point identified up to a maximum of three marks. (3)
- Christians believe that God created human life, thus making it sacred (1).
- Humans were made 'in the image of God' (Genesis 1:27) (1).
- Humans were made as the final special part of God's creation (1).
- Humans were given a soul to connect them to God (1).
- God is believed to have breathed life into humans (1).
Other valid answers will be accepted.
2 One mark will be awarded for providing each reason and a second mark for development of the reason up to a maximum of four marks. (4)
- The sanctity of life helps Christians to understand why they are a special part of God's creation (1). Unlike other creatures, they were made sacred 'in the image of God'. (Genesis 1:27) (1)
- It means Christians will value human life and this belief will affect how they act and behave (1). It will affect their views on issues such as abortion and euthanasia (1).
- It strengthens Christians' beliefs about the nature of God (1). They believe God is all-loving; creating humans to be special, holy and sacred reinforces this belief (1).
Other valid answers will be accepted.

29 Human origins

1 One mark will be awarded for providing each response and a second mark for development of the response up to a maximum of four marks. (4)
- Some Christians accept both the theory of evolution and the religious explanation provided in the Bible (1). They argue that evolution was part of God's plan to create humans (1).
- Some Christians believe they should reject the theory of evolution (1). Evolution contradicts the Bible's explanation of how humans were created (1).
Other valid answers will be accepted.
2 One mark will be awarded for providing each reason and a second mark for development of the reason up to a maximum of four marks. (4)
- Some Christians may believe that the theory of evolution contradicts the Bible's explanation of how God created humans (1). Evolution makes no reference to God (1).
- The theory of evolution suggests that humans were created by chance (1). This contradicts the Christian view that God planned and designed humans (1).
- It is difficult for Christians to believe the biblical Creation story is wrong, as the theory of evolution could undermine their belief in God's existence (1). Christians may feel that the scientific theory of evolution challenges their central source of authority and beliefs (1).
Other valid answers will be accepted.

30 Christian attitudes to abortion

1 "Christians should never support the use of abortion." Be sure to make your points specific, and refer to teachings and views, as you are instructed. You can support your arguments with biblical or other teachings. Make sure you give balanced views and then draw a conclusion – make sure you say why this is your conclusion. (12)
Arguments for the statement:
- All Christians accept that life is special/sacred/holy as it was created by God. Life is a gift that should be treasured and abortion does not support this idea.
- Some Christians believe that life begins at conception when a sperm fertilises an egg. This means that abortion is wrong and seen as murder, which is against the Ten Commandments: 'You shall not murder.' (Exodus 20:13)
- Many Christians believe that God has a plan and purpose for each and every life. Even if a child is likely to be born with substantial physical problems or is unlikely to survive, it is not a human's right to end that life through abortion. The only one who can make such decisions is God.
Arguments against the statement:
- Some Christians may accept certain situations where abortion is the 'lesser of two evils', for example in cases of pregnancy following rape or incest.
- Some Christians believe that as Jesus taught compassion towards others, this teaching should also be applied in certain cases of abortion. They believe that in circumstances where having a child might put the mother or other children at risk, abortion should be allowed.
- Some Christians believe that life does not necessarily begin at conception and therefore early abortions may be acceptable.
Other valid answers will be accepted.

31 Life after death (1)

1 One mark will be awarded for each point identified up to a maximum of three marks. (3)
- Christians believe that Jesus' resurrection proves there is life after death (1).
- Christians accept Bible teachings about a life after death (1).
- Christians believe Jesus taught of an afterlife as rooms in his father's house (1).
- Christians believe the purpose of life is a reward in heaven for living as God intended (1).

- Christians believe that the idea of reward and punishment makes sense and supports Christian teachings (1).

Other valid answers will be accepted.

2 One mark will be awarded for providing each reason and a second mark for development of the reason up to a maximum of four marks. (4)
- Christians believe that the afterlife is their ultimate reward for a life lived as God intended (1). This belief affects how they live, behave and act towards others, as they wish to achieve their eternal reward in heaven with God (1).
- A belief in life after death gives life on Earth meaning and purpose (1). It will affect every decision Christians make in trying to follow the example of Jesus so as to be rewarded in heaven (1).
- A belief in life after death gives hope and comfort (1). It helps Christians to cope with the sadness of death, as their loved ones are believed to live on (1).

Other valid answers will be accepted.

32 Life after death (2)

1 "Everyone should believe in life after death." Be sure to make your points specific, and refer to teachings and views, as you are instructed. You can support your arguments with biblical or other teachings. Make sure you give balanced views and then draw a conclusion – make sure you say why this is your conclusion. (12)

Arguments for the statement:
- Christians reject the idea that there is no evidence of life after death, as they accept the Bible's teaching about the resurrection of Jesus. They believe this is evidence that life after death exists and think that everyone should accept this as proof and live their lives accordingly.
- Christians reject the idea that life after death is just a form of social control, as they accept both the biblical description of heaven and hell and its explanation of what both are like in terms of being a place of reward or a place of eternal punishment. They feel that the idea of reward and punishment makes sense and so the afterlife is something that all people should believe in.
- Christians reject the Humanist idea that there is no life after death, as they believe that an all-loving God created the world and everything in it. An all-loving God wouldn't allow death to be the end, and having faith in this idea means putting trust in things that cannot necessarily be proved. They believe everyone should put their trust in God.

Arguments against the statement:
- Non-religious people accept that a belief in the afterlife can give people hope that death is not the end, but feel that this is a false sense of hope as there is no proof. They argue that the lack of scientific proof means that a belief in an afterlife should not be accepted.
- Many non-religious people feel that, in the past, before the development of scientific and empirical testing, ideas of an afterlife were used to control people and their behaviour. As society has changed and this is no longer necessary, they feel that there is now no need to believe in any sort of afterlife.
- Many non-religious people believe that some who claim to have contacted those who have died are fraudulent. As they have been shown to be con artists, they think a belief in the afterlife should not be accepted.

Other valid answers will be accepted.

33 Euthanasia

1 One mark will be awarded for each point identified up to a maximum of three marks. (3)
- Christians believe in the sanctity of life (1).
- Human life was created as a sacred gift from God (1).
- Euthanasia goes against the Commandment: 'You shall not murder' (Exodus 20:13) (1).
- Bible accounts, such as the story of Job, teach that suffering may have a purpose (1).

- Only God has the right to decide when life should end (1). Other valid answers will be accepted.

2 One mark will be awarded for providing each reason and a second mark for development of the reason up to a maximum of four marks. (4)
- Human life is a sacred gift from God (1). Christians believe they were made 'in the image of God.' (Genesis 1:27) (1)
- Christians do not accept murder (1). The Ten Commandments forbid murder and thus the taking of any human life. (Exodus 20:13) (1)
- Many Christians believe that hospices provide an alternative to euthanasia (1). Hospices provide palliative care so that a person can die with dignity (1).

Other valid answers will be accepted.

34 Issues in the natural world

1 "Christians have a duty to protect animals." Be sure to make your points specific, and refer to teachings and views, as you are instructed. You can support your arguments with biblical or other teachings. Make sure you give balanced views and then draw a conclusion – make sure you say why this is your conclusion. (12)

Arguments for the statement:
- Christians believe they were given stewardship, which is a God-given responsibility to care for the world. As animals are part of God's creation, Christians believe they should be protected.
- Christians see the world and everything in it – including animals – as a gift from God. They should therefore take care of this gift and not ruin it. Christians believe they will be judged in the afterlife on how they cared for the world, which includes how they treated animals.
- Christians believe that animals feel pain and therefore should be protected. Animals should not be exploited in experiments that are unnecessary or harmful to them.

Arguments against the statement:
- Many Christians believe that although humans have stewardship, they are allowed to use animals for food. As they believe God created animals for humans to use in this way, this is considered acceptable.
- Many Christians believe that if the use of animals in medical experiments means saving human life, this is acceptable. As only humans are created 'in the image of God' (Genesis 1:27), they are more important and so animals can be used for this purpose.
- Many Christians feel that animals were not given souls and therefore can be used by humans, but should not be exploited. This means they should be taken care of, but not given the same status as humans, who are considered more important.

Other valid answers will be accepted.

UNIT 5: CRIME AND PUNISHMENT

35 Justice

1 One mark will be awarded for each point identified up to a maximum of three marks. (3)
- Jesus taught that people should be treated fairly (1).
- God is seen to be just (1).
- Christians believe they will be judged after death (1).
- The biblical prophet Micah taught that God wants people to act justly (1).
- Christians believe in fair punishment as a form of justice (1).

Other valid answers will be accepted.

2 One mark will be awarded for providing each reason and a second mark for development of the reason up to a maximum of four marks. (4)
- Christians believe God always acts in a just and fair way, and they should follow his example. (1). The Church also teaches that people should behave justly towards others (1).

- Jesus taught about justice and treated people in a fair way (1). Christians believe that they should follow his example and 'do to others as you would have them do to you.' (Luke 6:31) (1)
- Bible teachings in passages such as Micah show that God wants people to act with justice and mercy (1): 'And what does the Lord require of you? To act justly and to love mercy and to walk humbly with your God.' (Micah 6:8) (1)

Other valid answers will be accepted.

36 Crime

1 One mark will be awarded for each point identified up to a maximum of three marks. (3)
- The Prison Fellowship organises victim awareness programmes (1).
- The Prison Fellowship supports the families of prisoners (1).
- The Prison Fellowship organises letter-writing programmes (1).
- The Prison Fellowship organises prayer groups and meetings (1).
- The Prison Fellowship donates money (1).

Other valid answers will be accepted.

2 One mark will be awarded for providing each teaching and a second mark for development of the teaching up to a maximum of four marks. (4)
- Christians believe that no one is free from sin and the Bible teaches people not to judge each other, but rather to help each other (1). This could be by giving money to charity, educating others or supporting those in prison (1).
- Christians believe in forgiveness for the sins of others as God forgives them their sins (1). They believe that working to achieve forgiveness between victims and criminals will lead to greater understanding and less reoffending (1).
- Christianity teaches that crime is wrong and against God's wishes, and Christians have a duty to resist it (1). The Ten Commandments contain rules from God, for example 'You shall not murder.' (Exodus 20:13) (1)

Other valid answers will be accepted.

37 Good, evil and suffering

1 "There is a reason why people suffer." Be sure to make your points specific, and refer to teachings and views, as you are instructed. You can support your arguments with biblical or other teachings. Make sure you give balanced views and then draw a conclusion – make sure you say why this is your conclusion. (12)

Arguments for the statement:
- Some Christians believe that evil and suffering is a part of life and there are Bible teachings that explain why people may suffer. The Parable of the Sheep and the Goats taught by Jesus teaches Christians about good and evil, and how they should help those in need in order to be rewarded in the afterlife.
- Many Christians believe that God gave humans free will and the right to make good or bad decisions. This means that humans are responsible for their own actions, including those that cause suffering.
- Some Christians believe that suffering is a test of their faith on Earth. The example of Job in the Bible, who suffered extensively, shows that there is sometimes a higher purpose to suffering – to test a person's belief and commitment to God.

Arguments against the statement:
- Atheists do not hold any religious beliefs and therefore do not accept that there is a divine reason why people suffer. They may even use suffering as an argument to suggest that God does not exist; if he did, he would want to stop people suffering.
- Humanists believe that humans have a degree of choice in their lives, and therefore are responsible for the choices they make. They do not believe that suffering is a test or part of a divine plan.

- Some people, including some Christians, believe that suffering is just a part of life and has no specific purpose. They may also believe that while suffering caused by natural 'evils', such as illness or famine, happens despite no one being at fault, humans should do what they can to reduce such suffering.

Other valid answers will be accepted.

38 Punishment

1 One mark will be awarded for each reason and a second mark for development of the reason up to a maximum of four marks. One further mark will be awarded for any relevant source of wisdom and authority. (5)
- God is presented in the Bible as a God of justice (1). Christians believe that God intends fair punishment as justice for a crime (1): 'The servant who knows the master's will and does not get ready or does not do what the master wants will be beaten with many blows.' (Luke 12:47) (1)
- Punishment is needed in society to maintain order and control (1). Christians believe that God commands people in the Bible to follow the laws of the country to achieve this (1): 'Let every person be subject to the governing authorities.' (Romans 13:1) (1)
- Christians believe that punishment is a way of giving criminals the opportunity to reform and earn forgiveness (1). Jesus taught about the importance of forgiveness when judging people, which allows them to change for the better (1): 'Be merciful, just as your Father is merciful … Do not judge, and you will not be judged. Do not condemn, and you will not be condemned. Forgive, and you will be forgiven.' (Luke 6:36–37) (1)

Other valid answers will be accepted.

39 Aims of punishment

1 "Reformation is the main aim of punishment." Be sure to make your points specific, and refer to teachings and views, as you are instructed. You can support your arguments with biblical or other teachings. Make sure you give balanced views and then draw a conclusion – make sure you say why this is your conclusion. (12)

Arguments for the statement:
- Christianity teaches that a key aim of punishment is giving criminals the opportunity to understand why their behaviour was wrong and to change by way of forgiveness. When Jesus was crucified on the cross, he even forgave those who punished him unfairly, giving them the opportunity to repent and reform.
- Christianity teaches that criminals deserve to be punished when they have committed a crime, but that they should be given support to help them change their behaviour. Christian organisations such as the Prison Fellowship support prisoners and their families, and reformation is an essential element of their work.
- Jesus taught about agape love: unconditional love that should be shown to all. Christians believe it should be shown to criminals to help them to repent and reform. Victim awareness programmes run by organisations such as the Prison Fellowship bring together victims and criminals to achieve deeper understanding and change.

Arguments against the statement:
- Other aims of punishment such as the protection of society may be considered more important. Human life is sacred as it was created by God, so violent or dangerous criminals should be kept away from society in order to protect it.
- Another aim of punishment is to prevent reoffending and to deter others from committing the same crimes. Christians agree that effective punishment should act as a deterrent and so help to reduce the level of crime.
- Justice is an important idea in Christianity, and making criminals pay for their crimes is considered an important aim of punishment. Old Testament teachings such as

'eye for eye, tooth for tooth' (Exodus 21:24) suggest that retribution is an accepted aim of punishment.
Other valid answers will be accepted.

40 Forgiveness

1 One mark will be awarded for each point identified up to a maximum of three marks. (3)
   • Christians believe Jesus died on the cross to bring forgiveness to the world (1).
   • Christians believe forgiveness helps to unite people as God intended (1).
   • Christians believe Jesus forgave others (1).
   • Christians believe forgiveness is the best way to achieve peace (1).
   • The Lord's Prayer shows that forgiveness is important (1).
   Other valid answers will be accepted.

2 One mark will be awarded for providing each teaching and a second mark for development of the teaching up to a maximum of four marks. (4)
   • One teaching is that Christians should forgive others as God has forgiven them (1). This is stated in the Lord's Prayer (1).
   • Christians believe that Jesus forgave those who put him to death on the cross (1): 'Father, forgive them, for they do not know what they are doing.' (Luke 23:34) (1)
   • The Bible teaches that reconciliation through forgiveness is the best way of resolving conflict (1): 'If you hold anything against anyone, forgive them.' (Mark 11:25) (1)
   Other valid answers will be accepted.

41 Treatment of criminals

1 One mark will be awarded for each point identified up to a maximum of three marks. (3)
   • Christians believe criminals should be treated with justice and fairness (1).
   • Most Christians believe that criminals should not be tortured (1).
   • Christians believe criminals should be given basic human rights (1).
   • Christians believe criminals have the right to a fair and unbiased trial (1).
   • Christians believe criminals should have the right to defend themselves (1).
   Other valid answers will be accepted.

2 One mark will be awarded for providing each reason and a second mark for development of the reason up to a maximum of four marks. (4)
   • The key Christian belief in the sanctity of life means that Christians believe criminals should be treated with justice (1). Christians believe all life is sacred as it was created by God – this is respected if criminals are treated fairly (1).
   • The Bible teaches that 'you are all one in Christ Jesus' (Galatians 3:28), meaning all humans deserve fair and just treatment as they are all of equal worth (1). God is seen to be just and fair, so Christians believe they should also act with justice towards others, including criminals (1).
   • Christianity teaches that all people deserve justice, and even criminals deserve just treatment in their right to a fair and unbiased trial (1). The Bible supports this right: 'Does our law condemn a man without first hearing him to find out what he has been doing?' (John 7:51) (1)
   Other valid answers will be accepted.

42 The death penalty

1 "Christians should support the death penalty." Be sure to make your points specific, and refer to teachings and views, as you are instructed. You can support your arguments with biblical or other teachings. Make sure you give balanced views and then draw a conclusion – make sure you say why this is your conclusion. (12)
   Arguments for the statement:
   • There are teachings in the Bible that appear to support the death penalty, making it acceptable as a form of punishment. Some Old Testament teachings such as 'eye for eye, tooth for tooth' (Exodus 21:24) can be interpreted to mean that if someone has taken the life of another, the death penalty would be acceptable.
   • The Church used the death penalty in the Middle Ages for those who opposed Christianity. This suggests that there are some crimes for which the death penalty could be acceptable.
   • St Paul teaches that a person should follow the laws of the country in which they live. If the UK government decided that the death penalty should be legalised for the most serious crimes, some Christians might feel they should support it: 'Let everyone be subject to the governing authorities.' (Romans 13:1)
   Arguments against the statement:
   • The death penalty doesn't allow time for forgiveness, which is a key Christian teaching. If a person receives the death penalty, they will not be given the opportunity to repent for what they have done wrong and to reform.
   • The death penalty goes against Christian ideas of love and compassion. Christianity teaches that people should 'do to others what you would have them do to you' (Matthew 7:12), which suggests that showing compassion and love is more important than revenge.
   • The death penalty goes against the key Christian teaching that human life is sacred as it was created by God. Taking any human life would be considered wrong, even if the person had committed a very serious crime.
   Other valid answers will be accepted.

UNIT 6: PEACE AND CONFLICT

43 Peace

1 One mark will be awarded for providing each reason and a second mark for development of the reason up to a maximum of four marks. (4)
   • Peace is important to Christians because it is a key teaching from Jesus. (1). This and other teachings are used to encourage people to live peacefully with each other (1).
   • Jesus taught the importance of peace in his Sermon on the Mount (1): 'Blessed are the peacemakers.' (Matthew 5:9) (1)
   • Jesus is promoted in the Bible as a peacemaker (1). Christians believe they should follow the example of Jesus' teachings and actions in order to live as God intended in the world (1).
   Other valid answers will be accepted.

2 One mark will be awarded for providing each reason and a second mark for development of the reason up to a maximum of four marks. (4)
   • Jesus taught the importance of peace in his Sermon on the Mount (1): 'Blessed are the peacemakers.' (Matthew 5:9) (1)
   • Jesus taught that people should treat others as they would like to be treated, and that they should live in peace with each other (1): 'Do to others as you would have them do to you.' (Luke 6:31) (1)
   • Jesus stopped the disciples from using violence in the Garden of Gethsemane (1). One of his disciples tried to defend him by striking the high priest and Jesus said 'No more of this!' (Luke 22:51) (1)
   Other valid answers will be accepted.

44 Peacemaking

1 One mark will be awarded for each point identified up to a maximum of three marks. (3)
   • Christian organisations educate people all around the world about the importance of peace (1).
   • Christian organisations hold interfaith conferences (1).
   • Christian organisations hold peace vigils (1).
   • Christian organisations teach people about forgiveness (1).
   • Christian organisations campaign against injustice (1).
   Other valid answers will be accepted.

2 One mark will be awarded for providing each reason and a second mark for development of the reason up to a maximum of four marks. (4)

- Christians believe that peace is what God intended for the world, with humans united and not divided (1). The Bible teaches that humans have a duty of stewardship to look after the world and this includes helping people to get along and to live peacefully together (1).
- Christians want to follow the example of Jesus who taught 'Blessed are the peacemakers' (Matthew 5:9) (1). Organisations such as the World Council of Churches try to put this into action by working for peace (1).
- The Church teaches that peace can be attained in the world through forgiveness and reconciliation between people (1). The Bible states: 'if you hold anything against anyone, forgive them.' (Mark 11:25) (1)

Other valid answers will be accepted.

45 Conflict

1 "Violence will never lead to peace in the world." Be sure to make your points specific, and refer to teachings and views, as you are instructed. You can support your arguments with biblical or other teachings. Make sure you give balanced views and then draw a conclusion – make sure you say why this is your conclusion. (12)

Arguments for the statement:

- Christians believe they have a duty to work to achieve world peace between people through non-violent means. This view is supported by many Bible teachings.
- Jesus taught that everyone has a responsibility to work for peace. He demonstrated this through the way he behaved and the teachings he gave Christians to follow – Christians such as Martin Luther King Jr have tried to do this.
- Some Christians are pacifists and believe that peace should be the ultimate goal. They would never use any violence to achieve this, believing instead that peace should be achieved through peaceful, non-violent means.

Arguments against the statement:

- Some non-religious people believe that peace cannot be achieved through non-violent methods. Although they accept that peace is important, they may believe that it can only be achieved through the use of violence.
- Some Christians may also accept that peace can sometimes only be achieved through violence but only after all other avenues have been explored. For example, the use of violence to remove a cruel dictator may be justified in order to protect innocent human life.
- Humanists may believe that violence is not advisable, but recognise that in some cases, such as the abuse of human rights during conflicts, violence can be the only way to achieve peace. They believe that human rights are important and that sometimes the right action is to use violence to stand up for them.

Other valid answers will be accepted.

46 Pacifism

1 One mark will be awarded for each point identified up to a maximum of three marks. (3)

- The Bible teaches that 'you shall not murder' (1).
- The New Testament teaches: 'put your sword back in its place' (Matthew 26:52) (1).
- Jesus taught people not to take revenge on others (1).
- Jesus taught 'love your neighbour as yourself' (Mark 12:31) (1).
- Jesus taught in the Sermon on the Mount 'Blessed are the peacemakers' (Matthew 5:9) (1).

Other valid answers will be accepted.

2 One mark will be awarded for each reason and a second mark for development of the reason up to a maximum of four marks. One further mark will be awarded for any relevant source of wisdom and authority. (5)

- Many of Jesus' teachings are about peace and Christians believe they should follow his example (1). Jesus is considered by some Christians to have been a pacifist (1), for example he taught: 'You have heard that it was said, "Love your neighbour and hate your enemy." But I tell you, love your enemies and pray for those who persecute you.' (Matthew 5:43–44) (1)
- The Bible contains many teachings that seem to support pacifism, suggesting that Christians should be pacifists (1). Christians recognise the need for peace and the importance of ending conflict by peaceful means (1): 'Put your sword back in its place … for all who draw the sword will die by the sword.' (Matthew 26:52) (1)
- Fighting involves threatening human life and is therefore wrong; life is seen to be sacred because it was created by God (1). Any use of violence threatens life, which also goes against teachings such as the Ten Commandments (1): 'You shall not murder.' (Exodus 20:13) (1)

Other valid answers will be accepted.

47 The Just War theory

1 "War is always wrong and can never be justified." Be sure to make your points specific, and refer to teachings and views, as you are instructed. You can support your arguments with biblical or other teachings. Make sure you give balanced views and then draw a conclusion – make sure you say why this is your conclusion. (12)

Arguments for the statement:

- Many Christians are pacifists and believe that no criteria for war can be given. They believe life is sacred as it was created as a gift from God. Threatening life in any way is therefore wrong, meaning war is wrong.
- Many Christians argue that war is wrong, as there are many Bible teachings that do not support war. Christianity promotes ideas of peace through Jesus and this is what Christians believe they should strive to achieve.
- Many Christians believe there is no justification for war – even based on the criteria of Just War theory. There are examples in history of people who used peaceful methods to achieve their goal – for example, Martin Luther King Jr – which shows that going to war is not necessary.

Arguments against the statement:

- Just War theory – where war is justified if certain criteria are met – has some support within Christianity. Some Christians believe that if a war is fought for the right reasons and under the right conditions, it may sometimes be necessary in order to achieve peace.
- Some Christians argue that war may be 'the lesser of two evils'. If, for example, war is the only option possible to defend a country or religion against an outside threat, it may be possible to justify it using Just War theory.
- Many Christian Churches, including the Catholic Church, accept Just War theory, meaning that war is sometimes right if all other options to restore peace and protect innocent life have failed.

Other valid answers will be accepted.

48 Holy war

1 One mark will be awarded for each point identified up to a maximum of three marks. (3)

- Christianity promotes ideas of peace (1).
- Some Bible passages suggest that war is sometimes acceptable (1).
- Some Christians are pacifists, believing war is always wrong (1).
- Some Christians believe war is acceptable if defending God (1).
- Christians believe Jesus was a peacemaker, the 'Prince of Peace' (1).

Other valid answers will be accepted.

2 One mark will be awarded for providing each teaching and a second mark for development of the teaching up to a maximum of four marks. (4)

- Christians teach ideas of peace, showing that war is wrong (1). Jesus taught about peace in his Sermon on the Mount: 'Blessed are the peacemakers.' (Matthew 5:9) (1)
- Some Bible passages, particularly in the Old Testament, teach that war may be acceptable as an act of retaliation (1): 'Whoever sheds human blood, by humans shall their blood be shed.' (Genesis 9:6) (1)
- New Testament teachings tend to suggest that war is wrong, as violence used in retaliation will only result in more violence (1): 'For all who draw the sword will die by the sword.' (Matthew 26:52) (1)

Other valid answers will be accepted.

49 Weapons of mass destruction

1 "The use of weapons of mass destruction can never be justified." Be sure to make your points specific, and refer to teachings and views, as you are instructed. You can support your arguments with biblical or other teachings. Make sure you give balanced views and then draw a conclusion – make sure you say why this is your conclusion. (12)

Arguments for the statement:

- Most Christians believe that the problems caused by weapons of mass destruction (WMD) outweigh any potential benefits. The devastation and loss of life that the use of WMD cause could never be justified, since human life, as created by God, is sacred.
- Christianity is a religion that promotes peace, therefore any use of WMD would be wrong. As WMD are indiscriminate in terms of targeting innocent life and causing damage to the environment, their use could never be justified.
- Many non-religious people would also not support the use of WMD due to the high loss of life. Even if not for religious reasons, they still recognise that life is special and should not be taken.

Arguments against the statement:

- Some people may recognise the benefits of having WMD, for example that wars can be won more quickly.
- If the aim of winning a war is to cause damage to the other side while inflicting as little harm as possible to your own side, it may be possible to justify the use of WMD.
- WMD can be used as a threat to hold over other nations without intending to actually use them. If they are only intended as a deterrent and are not to be used, this may be a way of justifying having the weapons.

Other valid answers will be accepted.

50 Issues surrounding conflict

1 One mark will be awarded for each point identified up to a maximum of three marks. (3)

- Christians can raise money to help those affected by conflict (1).
- Christians can hold prayer vigils (1).
- Christian charities can offer relief and medical help to those affected by conflict (1).
- Christians can volunteer and use their skills to help (1).
- Christians can raise awareness of conflict in the world and campaign for those in authority to work to end it (1).

Other valid answers will be accepted.

2 One mark will be awarded for providing each way and a second mark for development of the way up to a maximum of four marks. (4)

- Christians may work for peace by joining together with others as a community to work towards a common goal (1). Bible and Church teachings both advocate the end of conflict, and Christians would try to put this teaching into practice (1).
- When violence is used in the world, Christians may respond with peace vigils (1). For example, following terrorist

attacks, Christians have organised prayer events to pray for those affected (1).

- Christians may work to campaign against the use of violence and to persuade those in authority to act with compassion (1). They may take a pacifist approach of no violence, teaching that conflict should be ended through peaceful means (1).

Other valid answers will be accepted.

UNIT 7: PHILOSOPHY OF RELIGION

51 Revelation

1 One mark will be awarded for each point identified up to a maximum of three marks. (3)

- An example of revelation in the Bible is the covenant made between God and Noah (1).
- An example of revelation in the Bible is the covenant made between God and Abraham (1).
- An example of revelation in the Bible is seen in Jesus as God incarnate (1).
- An example of revelation in the Bible is the vision experienced by Saul/Paul (1).
- An example of revelation in the Bible is Joseph's dream (1).

Other valid answers will be accepted.

2 One mark will be awarded for providing each idea and a second mark for development of the idea up to a maximum of four marks. (4)

- In the Bible, God is shown to be omnipotent – all-powerful (1). This can be seen in the example of Noah. God was able to create a flood to destroy evil in the world, but he was also able to warn and save Noah and his family (1).
- God is shown to be omniscient (1). He is able to see and know everything that happens on Earth, as shown in the Bible story of Abraham and his son (1).
- God is shown to be benevolent (1). He cares for his creation, as shown in the way he communicates with humanity through examples such as Jesus and the prophets (1).

Other valid answers will be accepted.

52 Visions (1)

1 One mark will be awarded for each point identified up to a maximum of three marks. (3)

- An example of a vision in Christianity is that of Saul/Paul (1).
- An example of a vision in Christianity is that of St Bernadette (1).
- An example of a vision in Christianity is Joseph's dream (1).
- An example of a vision in Christianity is that of Moses (1).
- An example of a vision in Christianity is that of Abraham (1).

Other valid answers will be accepted.

2 One mark will be awarded for providing each reason and a second mark for development of the reason up to a maximum of four marks. (4)

- Visions help to show Christians the nature of God (1). For example, they show God is omnipotent as he has the power to connect with humanity through visions (1).
- Visions are a method that Christians believe God uses to communicate important messages to them (1). For example, Joseph received a vision from God that gave an important message to him about keeping Jesus safe (1).
- Visions show that God cares for his creation (1). The vision received by St Bernadette shows that God wanted to help humanity (1).

Other valid answers will be accepted.

53 Visions (2)

1 "Visions are proof of the existence of God." Be sure to make your points specific, and refer to teachings and views, as you are instructed. You can support your arguments with biblical or other teachings. Make sure you give balanced views and then draw a conclusion – make sure you say why this is your conclusion. (12)

Arguments for the statement:
- Christians may agree with this statement as they believe visions prove the existence of God. There are many examples in the Bible, the Christian holy book, such as the visions of Saul/Paul and Joseph. These help to confirm Christians' faith and enable them to better understand God.
- Visions also help to strengthen Christian beliefs about the nature of God. These include the idea that God is omnipotent, omniscient and benevolent. There are examples of visions that show both God's power and his love for his creation.
- Visions help Christians to get closer to God and to understand him better. Visions such as that received by Bernadette show that God cares about his creation and wants to interact and develop a relationship with humanity.

Arguments against the statement:
- Non-religious people are unlikely to accept that visions are proof of God's existence. They are unlikely to believe they are real and will offer alternative explanations for them, such as being the result of hallucinations or illness.
- Non-religious people may only accept experiences that can be verified scientifically. As many examples of possible visions happened long ago and cannot be scientifically tested, these people are unlikely to accept that they are real.
- Some Christians may not accept visions as evidence of God's existence. Although they believe in God and accept he exists, they may think that better evidence, such as miracles or the Bible itself, more fully reveals God than visions.

Other valid answers will be accepted.

54 Miracles

1 One mark will be awarded for each point identified up to a maximum of three marks. (3)
- A miracle in the Bible is Jesus walking on water (1).
- A miracle in the Bible is Jesus healing a blind man (1).
- A miracle in the Bible is the feeding of the 5000 (1).
- A miracle in the Bible is Jesus turning water into wine (1).
- A miracle in the Bible is the resurrection of Jesus (1).

Other valid answers will be accepted.

2 One mark will be awarded for each reason and a second mark for development of the reason up to a maximum of four marks. One further mark will be awarded for any relevant source of wisdom and authority. (5)
- Miracles reveal that God cares for his creation (1). For example, the healing miracles at Lourdes show that God wants to help humanity (1): 'The Lord remembers us and will bless us: he will bless his people Israel.' (Psalm 115:12) (1)
- Miracles can strengthen Christians' belief in God and help them to understand God better (1). Proof of God's existence and power is shown in the miracles performed by Jesus, for example in his walking on water (1): ' "Unless you people see signs and wonders," Jesus told him, "you will never believe".' (John 4:48) (1)
- Miracles are an important way for humanity to develop a relationship with God (1). God's miracles demonstrate that he is immanent and wants to be involved in the world, as in the example of Jesus' life and death (1): 'But God demonstrates his own love for us in this: while we were still sinners, Christ died for us.' (Romans 5:8) (1)

Other valid answers will be accepted.

55 Religious experiences

1 One mark will be awarded for each point identified up to a maximum of three marks. (3)
- Religious experiences are proof of God's existence (1).
- Religious experiences reveal what God is like (1).
- Religious experiences are a connection to God (1).
- Religious experiences can take the form of visions (1).
- Religious experiences can reveal a message from God (1).

Other valid answers will be accepted.

2 One mark will be awarded for providing each reason and a second mark for development of the reason up to a maximum of four marks. (4)
- Religious experiences reveal what God is like (1). The Bible story of Moses and the burning bush shows the power of God (1).
- Religious experiences offer a way for Christians to understand God better and to develop a relationship with him (1). The example of Jesus' life and death helps Christians to understand how much God loves his creation (1).
- Many examples of religious experience allow humanity to gain further knowledge about God (1). For example, the Bible story of Abraham's covenant with God shows that God is both transcendent and immanent (1).

Other valid answers will be accepted.

56 Prayers

1 One mark will be awarded for providing each reason and a second mark for development of the reason up to a maximum of four marks. One further mark will be awarded for any relevant source of wisdom and authority. (5)
- Prayers being answered will lead to a confirmation of faith that God exists (1). If a person asks for a miracle and it happens, it will reinforce their belief that God has heard their prayer and answered it (1): 'Therefore I tell you, whatever you ask for in prayer, believe that you have received it, and it will be yours.' (Mark 11:24) (1)
- Answered prayers help to confirm what God is like (1). They show Christians that God is benevolent and cares for his creation (1): 'But when you pray, go into your room, close the door and pray to your Father, who is unseen. Then your Father, who sees what is done in secret, will reward you.' (Matthew 6:6) (1)
- Answered prayers can help a person to develop a deeper relationship with God (1). Prayer is a way of communicating with him and understanding him better (1): 'This is the confidence we have in approaching God: that if we ask anything according to his will, he hears us.' (1 John 5:14) (1)

Other valid answers will be accepted.

57 The design argument

1 One mark will be awarded for each point identified up to a maximum of three marks. (3)
- God is the designer of the universe (1).
- God is the all-powerful creator of the universe (1).
- God showed benevolence in his plan and design for the world (1).
- God is transcendent in designing a world that is beyond human understanding (1).
- God is omniscient in foreseeing problems in his design for the world (1).

Other valid answers will be accepted.

2 One mark will be awarded for providing each idea and a second mark for development of the idea up to a maximum of four marks. (4)
- Christians may try to reconcile religious and scientific ideas about how the world was designed (1). They may claim that evolution was part of God's plan in designing the world (1).
- Christians may argue that there is too much evidence of a designer in the world (1). For example, the way the Earth is in orbit around the Sun or the way the tides move shows planning, rather than chance or luck, in their design (1).
- Christians may counter scientific arguments by claiming that science cannot explain everything about the world (1). Science may explain how the world was designed and created, but religion explains why and by whom the world was designed (1).

Other valid answers will be accepted.

58 The cosmological argument

1 "The cosmological argument proves God exists." Be sure to make your points specific, and refer to teachings and views, as you are instructed. You can support your arguments with biblical or other teachings. Make sure you give balanced views and then draw a conclusion – make sure you say why this is your conclusion. (12)

Arguments for the statement:
- Thomas Aquinas' version of the cosmological argument explained how everything in motion in the universe must have a first cause and why this cause has to be God. Many Christians accept this as proof that God exists.
- The cosmological argument helps to strengthen Christian faith as it reinforces the idea of God as omnipotent, benevolent and transcendent.
- The cosmological argument is able to respond to some of its critics. Its main challenger is the scientific theory of the 'Big Bang', which explains how the world came into existence without any reference to God. Christians may respond to this by arguing that God used the 'Big Bang' as part of his plan to create the world, thereby bringing scientific and religious explanations together to explain the origin of the universe.

Arguments against the statement:
- Non-religious people would not agree with the statement. They would argue that science explains how the world was created through the Big Bang, which means that no reference to God is needed. This means that the cosmological argument, which needs a first cause – or God – is wrong.
- Non-religious people may also challenge the cosmological argument by asking how God was created, as, if everything does have a cause, he cannot just have come into existence by himself. These are important issues to consider in this debate.
- Non-religious people may question why, if God created the world, there are examples of bad design such as earthquakes and volcanoes. This may damage the cosmological argument's claim that everything happens for a reason and has a purpose.

Other valid answers will be accepted.

59 Religious upbringing

1 One mark will be awarded for each point identified up to a maximum of three marks. (3)
- One feature of a religious upbringing is taking children to church on a Sunday (1).
- One feature is having children attend Sunday School (1).
- One feature is teaching children about Christianity (1).
- One feature is having a child baptised or christened (1).
- One feature is getting children to pray with their family (1).

Other valid answers will be accepted.

2 One mark will be awarded for providing each reason and a second mark for development of the reason up to a maximum of four marks. (4)
- If a person is brought up in the Christian faith, he or she is more likely to believe in God (1). They will have a good understanding of the Christian religion and be introduced to ideas about God from an early age (1).
- They will be introduced to God and to the Christian faith through baptism as a baby (1). If their parents raise them as Christians it is likely that they will confirm their faith in God through a confirmation ceremony when they are older (1).
- They will be introduced to the Christian community where they can find support and acceptance (1). This gives a sense of identity and belonging, in surroundings where they can find out more about God and socialise with people who share their ideas (1).

Other valid answers will be accepted.

UNIT 8: EQUALITY

60 Human rights

1 "Everyone deserves the same human rights." Be sure to make your points specific, and refer to teachings and views, as you are instructed. You can support your arguments with biblical or other teachings. Make sure you give balanced views and then draw a conclusion – make sure you say why this is your conclusion. (12)

Arguments for the statement:
- Christians believe key teachings from the Bible about how all humans are created by God in his image and Jesus' plea to 'treat others as you would like to be treated', which suggest that all humans should be treated equally and be given the same human rights in society.
- Christians such as Martin Luther King Jr and Desmond Tutu have stood up for human rights – they tried to ensure equality for all humans and put Christian teachings into action. Many Christians feel they should follow their example and stand up against injustice.
- Many non-religious people feel that human rights are important as they support ideas of equality and dignity. They believe that all people should have their human rights upheld and may therefore support action when these are at risk.

Arguments against the statement:
- Some people may not deserve to have all their human rights recognised. For example, criminals who have murdered someone and, therefore, taken away another person's right to life should have their own human rights limited (e.g. freedom).
- Some people may deserve to be treated differently in terms of equality and human rights. For example, people with disabilities may benefit from positive discrimination, and so treating them differently in some circumstances is acceptable.
- Some people in high-profile positions of authority both within and outside of religion or those who have put their own lives in danger by standing up for Christian principles against injustice may deserve special treatment in order to protect their human rights.

Other valid answers will be accepted.

61 Equality

1 One mark will be awarded for providing each solution and a second mark for development of the solution up to a maximum of four marks. (4)
- Some Christians, such as Martin Luther King Jr, have felt that they have a duty to work for equality. (1). He campaigned through petitions, speeches and the bus boycott for white and black people to be treated the same in society in mid-twentieth-century America (1).
- Christians may work with charities to reduce inequality. (1). Charities such as Christian Aid work to provide relief and aid following natural disasters (1).
- Many Christians work with those who need help to bring about a more equal society (1). They work with criminals and those living in poverty to help improve their situation (1).

Other valid answers will be accepted.

2 One mark will be awarded for providing each teaching and a second mark for development of the teaching up to a maximum of four marks. One further mark will be awarded for any relevant source of wisdom and authority. (5)
- The Bible teaches that all humans are made in the image of God (1). Christians believe humans are all God's creation and so should be treated with fairness and equality (1).
- The Bible teaches that God loves all people equally and does not show any favouritism towards anyone (1). After death he will also judge them with equal fairness (1): 'As for those who were held in high esteem – whatever they were makes no difference to me; God does not show favouritism – they added nothing to my message.' (Galatians 2:6) (1)
- Jesus treated all people equally, including those of lower standing in his society, such as women and people with leprosy (1). Christians believe they should follow his example and treat everyone as equals (1): 'So in Christ Jesus you are all children of God through faith, for all of you who were baptised into Christ have clothed yourselves with Christ.' (Galatians 3:26–27) (1)

Other valid answers will be accepted.

62 Religious freedom

1 One mark will be awarded for each point identified up to a maximum of three marks. (3)
- A multifaith society encourages greater tolerance of other religions (1).
- A benefit of living in a multifaith society is experiencing the traditions of other religions (1).
- A benefit of living in a multifaith society is greater unity among different religions (1).
- A benefit of living in a multifaith society is better understanding of other religious viewpoints (1).
- A benefit of living in a multi faith society is acceptance that all religions can co-exist peacefully (1).
Other valid answers will be accepted.

2 One mark will be awarded for providing each reason and a second mark for development of the reason up to a maximum of four marks. (4)
- The importance of being able to practise a religion freely is demonstrated through Jesus' teachings about equality and freedom (1). Teachings such as 'love your neighbour as yourself' (Mark 12:31) teach Christians how to behave towards others and to accept all religions (1).
- Christians believe it is important to show respect towards people of all religions (1). They believe all humans are made in the image of God and should be treated fairly regardless of their religion (1).
- Christians believe it is wrong to treat people differently because of their religion (1). Christianity teaches: 'There is neither Jew nor Gentile, neither slave nor free, nor is there male and female, for you are all one in Christ Jesus.' (Galatians 3:28) (1)
Other valid answers will be accepted.

63 Prejudice and discrimination

1 "All religions have equal value in today's world." Be sure to make your points specific, and refer to teachings and views, as you are instructed. You can support your arguments with biblical or other teachings. Make sure you give balanced views and then draw a conclusion – make sure you say why this is your conclusion. (12)
Arguments for the statement:
- Christians believe prejudice and discrimination are wrong. Many Christian teachings support this, such as 'treat others as you would like to be treated' or 'love your neighbour as yourself' (Mark 12:31).
- Christians accept that all humans have equal value as they were all created by God in his image. This means that no one should be treated differently for any reason.
- Christians follow the principle of agape love, which is unconditional love. Putting this into practice means not treating anybody differently for any reason, including their religion.
Arguments against the statement:
- Some Christians feel that if they agree with this statement, they are sidelining their own religion. Although they recognise some truths in other religions, they may support the view that Christianity should be the dominant religion.
- Some Christians accept that all people have equal value, but not that all religions do. They believe that Christianity is the only path that leads to God.
- Some Christians may feel that although other religions have partial truths, Christianity is the only completely true religion.
Other valid answers will be accepted.

64 Racial harmony

1 One mark will be awarded for each point identified up to a maximum of three marks. (3)
- A multi-ethnic society can encourage greater understanding between people from different backgrounds. (1).
- A multi-ethnic society can help to encourage respect between people (1).
- A multi-ethnic society can help to reduce discrimination (1).
- A multi-ethnic society brings a greater variety in food, music and culture (1).
- A multi-ethnic society can bring people together (1).
Other valid answers will be accepted.

2 One mark will be awarded for providing each way and a second mark for development of the way up to a maximum of four marks. (4)
- Christians such as Desmond Tutu campaigned for racial harmony in South Africa (1). He opposed the system of apartheid, which treated black and white people differently (1).
- Christians such as Martin Luther King Jr worked to achieve equality between black and white people in America (1). He marched, protested and held speeches to promote racial equality (1).
- Individual Christians have worked with international charities and other Christian organisations to educate others about racial harmony (1). Christians believe that teachings such as the Parable of the Good Samaritan show that all humans should be treated equally, regardless of race, and they try to put these teachings into practice (1).
Other valid answers will be accepted.

65 Racial discrimination

1 One mark will be awarded for providing each reason and a second mark for development of the reason up to a maximum of four marks. (4)
- Some Christians believe that a lack of respect can develop between different races (1). When people lose respect for each other, it can lead to a lack of understanding and unfair treatment (1).
- Christians may feel that minority groups can feel isolated in society (1). This reinforces social divisions between groups and promotes a lack of tolerance (1).
- When there is discrimination between different people, it can lead to unfairness in how resources are shared (1). This may mean that some groups do not receive what they are entitled to and this can lead to further bad feeling between people (1).
Other valid answers will be accepted.

2 One mark will be awarded for providing each teaching and a second mark for development of the teaching up to a maximum of four marks. One further mark will be awarded for any relevant source of wisdom and authority. (5)
- Christians follow the teaching 'love your neighbour as yourself' (Mark 12:31) and believe that everyone should be treated fairly (1). Christians believe that treating people differently because of their race goes against God's teachings (1).
- The Bible teaches that God made all humans in his own image (1). This shows that racial discrimination is wrong, as all humans should be treated the same (1): 'From one man he made all the nations.' (Acts 17:26) (1)
- Christians are taught by the Church that God loves everyone regardless of skin colour (1). St Paul teaches that there is no difference between humans (1): 'There is neither Jew nor Gentile, neither slave nor free, nor is there male and female, for you are all one in Christ Jesus.' (Galatians 3:28) (1)
- St Paul also teaches that God does not prefer one person to another (1). God is understood not to show favouritism towards people of one race over another (1): 'As for those who were held in high esteem – whatever they were makes no difference to me; God does not show favouritism.' (Galatians 2:6) (1)
Other valid answers will be accepted.

66 Social justice

1 "Everyone has a duty to work for social justice." Be sure to make your points specific, and refer to teachings and views, as you are instructed. You can support your arguments with biblical or other teachings. Make sure you give balanced views and then draw a conclusion – make sure you say why this is your conclusion. (12)

Arguments for the statement:
- Christians believe that they should follow teachings from the Bible such as 'love your neighbour as yourself' (Mark 12:31) and the example of Jesus who helped others. They feel they have a duty to work for social justice in the world, as this is what God wants.
- Christians believe that all humans were created by God and so all deserve equal treatment. They believe that all humans should have human rights and feel they have a responsibility to stand up for others when these rights are denied.
- Individual Churches have released statements responding to social justice issues. They believe people have a moral responsibility to ensure all humans are treated with equal respect and dignity, and have the rights to which they are entitled.

Arguments against the statement:
- If the theory of situation ethics is applied to situations of social justice, this may result in a different outcome in each given situation. As each situation is considered on its own merits, it may be the right thing to help someone in one situation but not in another.
- Sometimes Christians do not work actively for social justice because they believe they cannot make a difference as individuals. They may feel this task should be left to those in power, such as governments, who are more likely to be able to bring about social change.
- Some Christians believe that the best way to help others is to encourage them to be self-reliant and to help themselves. They accept that they may not always understand God's purpose for humans in the world, but that sometimes it is not their duty to help others.

Other valid answers will be accepted.

67 Wealth and poverty

1 One mark will be awarded for each point identified up to a maximum of three marks. (3)
   - Christians can support charities such as Christian Aid (1).
   - Christians can tithe (1).
   - Christians can volunteer (1).
   - Christians can support food banks (1).
   - Christians can share what they have with others (1).
   Other valid answers will be accepted.

2 One mark will be awarded for providing each reason and a second mark for development of the reason up to a maximum of four marks. (4)
   - The Bible teaches that after death God will judge humans on how they treated others, including how they helped those in poverty (1). The Parable of the Sheep and the Goats explains this (1): 'He will separate the people one from another as a shepherd separates the sheep from the goats. He will put the sheep on his right and the goats on his left.' (Matthew 25:32–33)
   - Christians believe that they should follow the example of Jesus by helping those in poverty as he helped others (1). Jesus showed care and compassion towards others, especially those who were sick, poor or shunned by the rest of society, such as lepers (1).
   - Christians support charities such as Christian Aid that work to help others and put Christian teachings into action in order to help those living in poverty (1). Christian Aid puts 'treat others as you would like to be treated' into practice (1)
   Other valid answers will be accepted.

Islam

UNIT 1: MUSLIM BELIEFS
68 The Six Beliefs of Islam

1 One mark will be awarded for each point identified up to a maximum of three marks. (3)
   - One feature of the Six Beliefs of Sunni Islam is belief in one God (1).
   - One feature of the Six Beliefs is belief in angels (1).
   - One feature of the Six Beliefs is the authority of holy books (1).
   - One feature of the Six Beliefs is prophethood (1).
   - One feature of the Six Beliefs is the belief in predestination (1).
   - One feature of the Six Beliefs is belief in life after death (1).
   Other valid answers will be accepted.

2 One mark will be awarded for providing each reason and a second mark for development of the reason up to a maximum of four marks. (4)
   - The Six Beliefs help all Sunni Muslims to better understand their religion, Islam. For example, they all accept the belief that there is one God called Allah (1).
   - They show Sunni Muslims how to live their lives (1) according to Allah's rules. For example, one of the Six Beliefs is the belief in life after death, which affects how Muslims behave and and how they treat others so that they will be rewarded in the afterlife (1).
   - They are the basic principles of Islam accepted by all Sunni Muslims (1). For example, all Sunni Muslims recognise the importance of prophethood as God's way of communicating with humanity (1).
   Other valid answers will be accepted.

69 The five roots of 'Usul ad-Din in Shi'a Islam

1 One mark will be awarded for providing each reason and a second mark for development of the reason up to a maximum of four marks. (4)
   - The five roots of 'Usul ad-Din are all based on the concept of Tawhid (the oneness of Allah) (1). For example, everything a Muslim does is linked to the concept of submitting to Allah in all aspects of their life (1).
   - Tawhid is important because Muslim prayers are directed five times a day to Allah (1). Regular communication addressed to Allah through prayer helps Muslims to understand him better (1).
   - Tawhid is a central idea in Islam and is given prominence in the Qur'an through Surah 112 (1). This refers to Allah as: 'The Self-Sufficient Master, Whom all creatures need.' (Surah 112:2) (1)
   Other valid answers will be accepted.

2 One mark will be awarded for providing each root and a second mark for development of the root up to a maximum of four marks. (4)
   - One of the five roots of 'Usul ad-Din is Tawhid (1), the oneness of God called Allah (1).
   - One of the five roots of 'Usul ad-Din is Adl (1). Muslims believe Allah is fair and just in his treatment of everything (1).
   - One of the five roots of 'Usul ad-Din is Nubuwwah (1). This is the belief in prophets appointed by Allah to pass on messages to humanity (1).
   Other valid answers will be accepted.

70 The nature of Allah

1 One mark will be awarded for each point identified up to a maximum of three marks. (3)
   - Muslims believe Allah is transcendent (1).
   - Muslims believe Allah is merciful (1).
   - Muslims believe Allah is immanent (1).
   - Muslims believe Allah will judge humans after death (1).
   - Muslims believe Allah is loving (1).
   Other valid answers will be accepted.

2 One mark will be awarded for providing each way and a second mark for development of the way up to a maximum of four marks. One further mark will be awarded for any relevant source of wisdom and authority. (5)
   - Allah is described in the Qur'an as being transcendent, beyond human understanding (1). Muslims use his 99 names to help them understand what he is like (1): 'And the

Most Beautiful Names belong to Allah, so call on Him by them.' (Surah 7:180) (1)

- Allah is described using the term Tawhid (1), meaning that he is the one God and Muslims should worship only him (1): 'Worship Allah, and avoid Taghut.' (Surah 16:36) (1)
- Allah is described as merciful (1). Muslims believe Allah will forgive them after death if they are sorry for what they have done wrong (1): 'verily Allah forgives all sins. Truly, He is Oft-Forgiving, Most Merciful.' (Surah 39:53) (1)

Other valid answers will be accepted.

71 Risalah

1 One mark will be awarded for each point identified up to a maximum of three marks. (3)
- Prophets are important in Islam as they are messengers of Allah (1).
- Prophets are important as they allow Allah to communicate with humans (1).
- Some prophets are important because they have brought written messages (1).
- Prophets are important as they have shown humans how Allah wants them to live (1).
- Some prophets are important because they have brought warnings from Allah (1).

Other valid answers will be accepted.

2 One mark will be awarded for providing each reason and a second mark for development of the reason up to a maximum of four marks. (4)
- Prophets are important in Islam as Allah uses them to communicate with humanity (1). For example, Ibrahim carried messages from Allah to encourage people to worship God (1).
- Some prophets are important as they have brought holy books from Allah (1), for example Muhammad brought the Qur'an (1).
- Prophets act as examples of how Allah wants Muslims to live their lives (1). Isma'il showed the characteristics of patience and compassion that Muslims should try to develop (1).

Other valid answers will be accepted.

72 Muslim holy books

1 One mark will be awarded for each point identified up to a maximum of three marks. (3)
- The Qur'an was revealed to Muhammad (1).
- It was revealed over 23 years (1).
- The Qur'an is divided into chapters and verses (1).
- Muslims believe the Qur'an came from Allah (1).
- The Qur'an is written in Arabic (1).

Other valid answers will be accepted.

2 One mark will be awarded for providing each reason and a second mark for development of the reason up to a maximum of four marks. (4)
- The Qur'an is important because it is believed to have come directly from Allah (1). Allah revealed it through the angel Jibril (1).
- The Qur'an is used by Muslims in prayer and worship (1). The Imam recites passages from the Qur'an during worship in the mosque (1).
- Muslims believe the Qur'an is a form of revelation of Allah (1). It reveals to Muslims that Allah is all-powerful and loving (1).

Other valid answers will be accepted.

73 Malaikah

1 "Belief in angels is the most important belief in Islam." Be sure to make your points specific, and refer to teachings and views, as you are instructed. You can support your arguments with Qur'anic or other teachings. Make sure you give balanced views and then draw a conclusion – make sure you say why this is your conclusion. In this question, 3 of the marks awarded will be for your spelling, punctuation and grammar, and your use of specialist terminology. (15)

Arguments for the statement:
- A belief in angels is important because Muslims believe Allah uses them to communicate with humans. For example, angels have been used in Islam to pass messages to the prophets, such as when Muhammad received the Qur'an from the angel Jibril.
- Angels in Islam are important as they have significant roles. For example, the Qur'an explains that Izra'il is the angel of death and helps Muslims to understand that they need to live their lives as Allah wishes.
- Important teachings about angels offer proof to Muslims that there is an afterlife. Muslims wish to be rewarded in the afterlife and not punished, so the teaching of Mika'il (the angel of mercy) reassures them that this is possible.

Arguments against the statement:
- Some Muslims accept that a belief in angels is important but do not believe that it is the most important belief in Islam. At the centre of Islam is the belief that Muslims should submit to Allah in all aspects of their lives. This could be considered more important as it underpins all other beliefs.
- Some Muslims would argue that all beliefs in Islam are important and no 'one' belief is more important than another. For example, key Muslim beliefs include belief in the afterlife, belief in Allah and belief in prophethood, which all have equal importance.
- Some Muslims hold that while belief in angels is important, it may be more important to consider how Allah wants them to live their own lives. Putting beliefs into practice may be considered more important as it impacts on their afterlife as well as pleasing Allah.

Other valid answers will be accepted.

74 Al-Qadr

1 One mark will be awarded for each point identified up to a maximum of three marks. (3)
- Muslims believe that Allah controls everything (1).
- Al-Qadr is predestination (1).
- Muslims believe that al-Qadr is linked to the Day of Judgement (1).
- Al-Qadr is one of the Six Beliefs for Sunni Muslims (1).
- Shi'a Muslims do not accept al-Qadr (1).

Other valid answers will be accepted.

2 One mark will be awarded for providing each way and a second mark for development of the way up to a maximum of four marks. (4)
- Having a belief in al-Qadr (predestination) means that Muslims accept the idea of living their lives according to what Allah wants (1). Muslims want to be rewarded in heaven rather than punished in hell (1).
- Holding a belief in al-Qadr will make Muslims aware of every action they perform (1). They will want to follow the rules of Allah, for example the Five Pillars (1).
- A belief in al-Qadr will encourage Muslims to want to help others (1). They believe that behaving in this way, which is commanded in the Qur'an by Allah, will help them to gain favour with him (1).

Other valid answers will be accepted.

75 Akhirah

1 One mark will be awarded for each point identified up to a maximum of three marks. (3)
- After death, the angel of death takes a person's soul to barzakh (1).
- Islam teaches that Muslims will be judged after death by Allah (1).
- Muslims believe that they can be rewarded in paradise (1).
- Muslims believe that they can be punished in hell (1).
- Muslims believe that they will be judged on how they have lived their lives (1).

Other valid answers will be accepted.

One mark will be awarded for providing each way and a second mark for development of the way up to a maximum of four marks. (4)

- Both Muslims and Christians accept the idea of life being a test for the afterlife (1). They both accept that, after death, humans will be judged by God on how they have lived their lives and behaved towards others (1).
- Both Muslims and Christians accept the idea of eternal reward or punishment after death (1). They both accept the idea of the reward of heaven or paradise for those who have been good and the punishment of hell for those who have sinned (1).
- Both Muslims and Christians accept the idea of resurrection (1). They do not believe that death is the end but that the soul and body are reunited in the afterlife (1).

Other valid answers will be accepted.

UNIT 2: MARRIAGE AND THE FAMILY

76 Marriage

1 One mark will be awarded for each point identified up to a maximum of three marks. (3)
- Marriage is intended to be for life (1).
- Marriage is viewed as a legal contract (1).
- Marriage is between a man and a woman (1).
- Muslim women are expected to only marry Muslim men (1).
- Muslim men may marry up to four wives (1).

Other valid answers will be accepted.

2 One mark will be awarded for providing each reason and a second mark for development of the reason up to a maximum of four marks. (4)
- Marriage is important to Muslims as it is believed to be the correct context in which to have a family (1). Muslims are expected to get married and to raise their children within the Islamic faith (1).
- Marriage is a duty commanded by Allah (1). The Qur'an commands: 'marry those among you who are single.' (Surah 24:32) (1)
- Muslims believe marriage is a stable and strong foundation for society (1). The family unit created within marriage is believed to be a place for the teaching of morals and the difference between right and wrong (1).

Other valid answers will be accepted.

77 Sexual relationships

1 One mark will be awarded for each point identified up to a maximum of three marks. (3)
- Muslims believe sex is an act of worship (1).
- Islam teaches that sexual relationships should only take place within marriage (1).
- Islam teaches that sexual relationships are intended to fulfil physical, emotional and spiritual needs (1).
- Islam teaches that sex is a gift from Allah (1).
- Islam teaches that adultery is always wrong (1).

Other valid answers will be accepted.

2 One mark will be awarded for providing each reason and a second mark for development of the reason up to a maximum of four marks. One further mark will be awarded for any relevant source of wisdom and authority. (5)
- Muslims believe that Allah intended sex to take place only within marriage (1). Sex is intended as a gift from Allah for married couples (1): 'When a husband and wife share intimacy it is rewarded, and a blessing from Allah; just as they would be punished if they had engaged in illicit sex.' (Hadith) (1)
- The Qur'an forbids adultery (1) because sex outside of marriage is seen to break the special relationship between husband and wife (1): 'Nor come nigh to adultery: for it is a shameful deed and an evil, opening the road to other evils.' (Surah 17:32) (1)

- Only sex within marriage is regarded as the correct context in which a husband and wife can satisfy each other's physical, emotional and spiritual needs (1). Islam teaches that this is a duty from Allah and should occur exclusively between a husband and wife (1): 'When a husband and wife share intimacy it is rewarded, and a blessing from Allah.' (Hadith) (1)

Other valid answers will be accepted.

78 Families

1 "The most important purpose of family for Muslims is to strengthen the ummah." Be sure to make your points specific, and refer to teachings and views, as you are instructed. You can support your arguments with Qur'anic or other teachings. Make sure you give balanced views and then draw a conclusion – make sure you say why this is your conclusion. (12)

Arguments for the statement:
- Some Muslims agree with the statement as Muslim families often attend the mosque together. This helps to unite all Muslims as they recognise that they are all praying together at the same time each day. Individual family units can feel that they have support and are part of the worldwide ummah through this shared worship.
- The family unit celebrates important occasions such as Eid and rites of passage such as the birth of a child or the joining of families in marriage. This helps to strengthen the ummah. The local community comes together for these events, demonstrating that there is unity between all Muslims.
- The ummah has great importance in Islam, with the family being recognised as the first level of the community. The Qur'an teaches that Muslims should be united: 'And hold fast, all of you together, to the Rope of Allah' (Surah 3:103) – a united family unit helps to reinforce and support this teaching.

Arguments against the statement:
- Although strengthening the ummah is recognised by Muslims as important, other more practical purposes of the family unit may be considered more important. Another purpose of the family is to care for all of its members; teachings from the Qur'an reinforce the importance of taking care of each other, especially more elderly relatives.
- Some Muslims may feel that a more important purpose of the family is the education of the young. The family is where children are taught about their faith and the religion of Islam. They are taught how to pray and to follow the rules of Islam; this is an important purpose of the family.
- Some Muslims may feel that the family is a private unit where people can support, care and love each other. Although the worldwide ummah is recognised as an essential part of Islam, the smaller family unit is where teachings such as respecting and obeying parents are put into practice. This has a steadying and stabilising impact on the whole of society.

Other valid answers will be accepted.

79 The family in the ummah

1 One mark will be awarded for each point identified up to a maximum of three marks. (3)
- It is the duty of the ummah as Muslims to care for each other (1).
- It shows unity between all Muslims (1).
- It is a Muslim duty to provide guidance for the family in times of conflict (1).
- Muslims believe that support from the ummah will lead to successful Muslim families who will, in turn, give stability to society (1).
- It strengthens the ummah (1).

Other valid answers will be accepted.

2 One mark will be awarded for providing each way and a second mark for development of the way up to a maximum of four marks. (4)

- Muslims in the community can encourage families to worship together in their local mosque (1). This will unite them in a common shared goal of worshipping Allah (1).
- The local community can provide parenting classes to support the family unit (1). These classes give parents guidance and support in how to raise their children (1).
- The local community can provide counselling (1). This allows all members of the family unit to work together to resolve any issues (1).

Other valid answers will be accepted.

80 Contraception

1 "Muslims should not use contraception." Be sure to make your points specific, and refer to teachings and views, as you are instructed. You can support your arguments with Qur'anic or other teachings. Make sure you give balanced views and then draw a conclusion – make sure you say why this is your conclusion. (12)

Arguments for the statement:
- Some Muslims believe that they should only use natural methods of contraception as promoted in some sources of authority in Islam. The use of artificial methods of contraception is not permitted.
- Muslims believe that the purpose of sex is procreation – to have a family. Some Muslims believe that as permanent methods of contraception prevent this, they should not be used.
- Many Muslims believe that having a family is a duty from Allah and so using contraception goes against this: 'when a husband and wife share intimacy it is rewarded, and a blessing from Allah.' (Hadith)

Arguments against the statement:
- Some Muslims believe that contraception can be used if there is a valid reason. This may include situations where the life of the mother could be at risk if she were to have a child; in this case, the use of contraception would be justified.
- Some Muslims argue that using contraception in order to preserve current children would be a valid reason. If the wellbeing of the current family unit is protected through a couple using contraception, this would justify its use.
- There are examples in Sahih al-Bukhari which teach that, in the time of Muhammad, natural forms of contraception were commonly used and so may be acceptable: 'we used to practise coitus interruptus during the lifetime of Allah's Apostle.'

Other valid answers will be accepted.

81 Divorce

1 One mark will be awarded for providing each reason and a second mark for development of the reason up to a maximum of four marks. (4)
- Muhammad taught that divorce should be a last resort (1). The couple are expected to try to reconcile before considering divorce (1).
- Divorce is considered detestable by Allah (1). The Qur'an teaches that it is the most hated of all acts to Allah (1).
- Marriage is intended to be for life (1). When a Muslim couple marry, they enter the union believing that it should last forever (1).

Other valid answers will be accepted.

2 One mark will be awarded for providing each reason and a second mark for development of the reason up to a maximum of four marks. One further mark will be awarded for any relevant source of wisdom and authority. (5)
- The Qur'an has strict guidelines on what should happen if a couple are considering divorce (1). Part of this process is the iddah, where there is a waiting period to see if a couple can reconcile (1): 'if they return (change their idea in this period), verily, Allah is Oft-Forgiving, Most Merciful.' (Surah 2:226) (1)

- Some Muslims are realistic and know that relationships can break down (1). As Muslims often have arranged marriages there may be issues within a relationship that can lead to divorce (1): 'And if they decide upon divorce, then Allah is All-Hearer, All-Knower.' (Surah 2:227) (1)
- Shari'ah law teaches that divorce is allowed (1). Islam understands marriage to be a contract, so it can be ended (1): 'Then when they are about to fulfil their term appointed, either take them back in a good manner or part with them in a good manner.' (Surah 65:2)

Other valid answers will be accepted.

82 Men and women in the family

1 "Muslim men and women have equal roles in the family." Be sure to make your points specific, and refer to teachings and views, as you are instructed. You can support your arguments with Qur'anic or other teachings. Make sure you give balanced views and then draw a conclusion – make sure you say why this is your conclusion. (12)

Arguments for the statement:
- Muslims accept that men and woman have equal roles in the family, although these roles are different. Traditionally, men are seen as the providers and protectors, while women are the carers in the family and home.
- Teachings from the Qur'an support the view of men and women having equality in the family: Surah 4 teaches that men and women were created 'from a single person' (Surah 4:1), which suggests equality, although this does not mean that they perform the exact same roles within the family unit.
- Muhammad stood up for equality between men and women and his teaching supports the view of men and women having equal roles within the family. He taught that men and women were 'equal like the teeth of a comb' (Hadith), suggesting that although they perform different roles within the family, these roles complement each other.

Arguments against the statement:
- Some quotes in the Qur'an suggest there is inequality between men and women, supporting the view that women in the family must submit to their husbands: 'men are in charge of women' (Surah 4:34). This suggests that the roles of men and women are not equal and that men have power over women.
- In the time of Muhammad, it is believed he witnessed many examples of inequality between men and women in the family. This may, for some Muslims, justify women not being seen or treated as equal within the family unit today.
- In Islam, men and women are viewed by Muslims to be equal but not the same. Men are seen as the providers within the family unit, while women are regarded as the home-keepers and carers for children.

Other valid answers will be accepted.

83 Gender prejudice and discrimination

1 One mark will be awarded for each point identified up to a maximum of three marks. (3)
- Malala Yousafzai stood up against the Taliban to achieve equality in education (1).
- Nadiya Hussain has raised awareness of the importance of gender equality (1).
- Sisters in Islam challenge the mistreatment of women (1).
- The Inclusive Mosque Initiative works for equality in prayer (1).
- Many Muslims work to educate others about gender equality in Islam (1).

Other valid answers will be accepted.

2 One mark will be awarded for providing each reason and a second mark for development of the reason up to a maximum of four marks. (4)
- Islam teaches that men and women should be treated the same way (1). Muslims believe Allah created all humans to be equal (1).

- Muslims believe that after death Allah will judge men and women in the same way (1). They believe that if a person – male or female – has acted as Allah wishes, they will be rewarded with entry to heaven (1).
- Men and women have the same rights and responsibilities (1), for example men and women are both expected to get married (1).

Other valid answers will be accepted.

UNIT 3: LIVING THE MUSLIM LIFE

84 The Ten Obligatory Acts of Shi'a Islam

1 One mark will be awarded for each point identified up to a maximum of three marks. (3)
- One purpose of the Ten Obligatory Acts is to guide Shi'a Muslims in how they live their lives (1).
- One purpose is to allow them to get closer to Allah (1).
- One purpose is to help them reach paradise after death (1).
- One purpose is to help them continually focus their actions on Allah (1).
- One purpose is to unite all Shi'a Muslims in their shared beliefs (1).

Other valid answers will be accepted.

2 One mark will be awarded for providing each way and a second mark for development of the way up to a maximum of four marks. (4)
- Muslims must pray five times a day as one of the Ten Obligatory Acts (1). They believe that regular communication with Allah through daily worship fulfils the duty of Salah, which is one of the Ten Obligatory Acts (1).
- Muslims try to resist temptations that may challenge them in their daily lives. (1) This could include not lying, swearing or harming others (1).
- Muslims fast during the month of Ramadan (1). During this time, they do not eat or drink during daylight hours (1).

Other valid answers will be accepted.

85 The Shahadah

1 One mark will be awarded for each point identified up to a maximum of three marks. (3)
- The Shahadah contains the fundamental belief that there is one God (1).
- The Shahadah contains the important belief that Muhammad is the prophet of Islam (1).
- The Shahadah is accepted by all Muslims (1).
- Muslims recite the Shahadah daily as a declaration of their faith (1).
- Reciting the Shahadah is seen to demonstrate commitment to the religion of Islam (1).

Other valid answers will be accepted.

2 One mark will be awarded for providing each way and a second mark for development of the way up to a maximum of four marks. (4)
- The Shahadah is whispered into the ears of newborn babies (1). Muslims believe it is important that the first thing a baby hears is the idea of belief in one God, Allah (1).
- Muslims believe it is important to say the Shahadah aloud in front of witnesses (1). This is done publicly so Muslims can show that they accept their religion, meaning they believe in Allah and Muhammad (1).
- Muslims recite and hear the Shahadah daily (1). It is part of the adhan – the daily call to prayer (1).

Other valid answers will be accepted.

86 Salah

1 "Salah is the most important of the Five Pillars for Muslims." Be sure to make your points specific, and refer to teachings and views, as you are instructed. You can support your arguments with Qur'anic or other teachings. Make sure you give balanced views and then draw a conclusion – make sure you say why this is your conclusion. In this question, 3 of the marks awarded will be for your spelling, punctuation and grammar, and your use of specialist terminology. (15)

Arguments for the statement:
- Salah is compulsory prayer five times a day, which demonstrates regular communication with Allah. As it is one of the Five Pillars – which are duties – and it happens most frequently, some Muslims could consider it to be the most important of all the pillars.
- In performing Salah, all Muslims complete this pillar at the same time each day, facing the same way and performing the same actions, therefore uniting and strengthening the ummah. This might make it the most important pillar. Its importance is also shown through group communal prayer in the Jummah service, which takes place on a Friday in the mosque and which all Muslims strive to attend to show commitment to the ummah.
- Muhammad, as the prophet of Allah, established Salah and this shows its importance. The Qur'an states that Muhammad was the one who established prayer (Surah 29:45), demonstrating that he gave this special significance among the Five Pillars.

Arguments against the statement:
- Muslims might consider that no pillar is more important than any of the others. The basic beliefs and duties of Islam, collected together as the Five Pillars, are all equally important and Muslims believe all should be performed for Allah.
- Some Muslims may believe that Zakah and Sawm have more of a practical impact in the world and strengthen the ummah in a greater way than the other pillars. As Zakah and Sawm can involve helping others in the community through sharing money and food, they could be considered more important.
- Shahadah – the declaration of faith and the first Pillar of Islam – could be considered more important than prayer. Islam is understood by Muslims to mean 'submission to Allah', and as the Shahadah contains the belief that there is no God but Allah, it underpins all the other pillars and is regarded as most important for many Muslims.

Other valid answers will be accepted.

87 Sawm

1 One mark will be awarded for each point identified up to a maximum of three marks. (3)
- Muslims who are sick may be excused from fasting (1).
- Those who are elderly may be excused from fasting (1).
- Young children are excused from fasting (1).
- Pregnant women are excused from fasting (1).
- Those travelling on long journeys are excused from fasting (1).

Other valid answers will be accepted.

2 One mark will be awarded for providing each reason and a second mark for development of the reason up to a maximum of four marks. (4)
- Sawm is one of the Five Pillars and is therefore a duty (1). Fasting during Ramadan shows obedience to Allah (1).
- Performing Sawm shows self-discipline (1). Muslims must not eat during daylight hours, which shows that they are willing to suffer for Islam (1).
- Performing Sawm helps Muslims to remember the significance of the month of Ramadan in Islam (1). This was when the Qur'an was revealed to Muhammad from Allah (1).

Other valid answers will be accepted.

88 Zakah and khums

1 One mark will be awarded for each point identified up to a maximum of three marks. (3)
- Zakah is 2.5 per cent of a Muslim's annual wealth (1).
- Zakah is used to help the poor (1).
- Zakah is a duty in Islam (1).

- Zakah happens once a year (1).
- The act of giving Zakah is seen to strengthen and support the ummah (1).

Other valid answers will be accepted.

2 One mark will be awarded for providing each reason and a second mark for development of the reason up to a maximum of four marks. (4)
- Khums is important as it is used to directly support Muhammad's descendants and the leaders that Shi'a Muslims recognise as following him (1). The Qur'an details who should receive khums and how the money should be shared out (Surah 8) (1).
- Khums is important as it can be used to help those studying the religion of Islam (1). Khums is therefore used to benefit the whole religion of Islam, which in turn strengthens the ummah (1).
- Giving khums is important as Shi'a Muslims believe it is a duty (1). Shi'a Muslims recognise it as one of the Ten Obligatory Acts (1).

Other valid answers will be accepted.

89 Hajj

1 "The benefits of attending Hajj outweigh the challenges." Be sure to make your points specific, and refer to teachings and views, as you are instructed. You can support your arguments with Qur'anic or other teachings. Make sure you give balanced views and then draw a conclusion – make sure you say why this is your conclusion. In this question, 3 of the marks awarded will be for your spelling, punctuation and grammar, and your use of specialist terminology. (15)

Arguments for the statement:
- Hajj is one of the Five Pillars of Islam and is therefore a duty commanded by Allah, as seen in Surah 22. Muslims believe that by completing Hajj, they are demonstrating their commitment to Allah and to the religion of Islam.
- All Muslims are expected to try to complete Hajj once in their lifetime and it reinforces the view that all Muslims belong to the ummah. Completing Hajj reinforces ideas of equality with all Muslims wearing the same clothing and performing the same actions at the same time, so helping them to feel united and strengthening the ummah.
- Hajj is important for reminding Muslims of significant historical events in the religion of Islam detailed in the Qur'an (Surah 2). While completing this pillar, Muslims have the opportunity to focus on their religion, spending time in reflection and asking Allah for forgiveness, which is considered important if they are to achieve paradise after death.

Arguments against the statement:
- Muslims are expected to be physically fit and financially stable in order to complete Hajj and this can be a great challenge for some. Muslims may feel that they have failed Allah if they are not able to perform all Five Pillars, which are viewed as duties in the religion of Islam.
- One of the challenges of Hajj today is that it has become more popular, leading to over two million pilgrims attending every year. This can detract from the specialness of this event. Some Muslims may feel that there are too many people present to be able to have the personal experience of Allah they hope to achieve by completing this pillar.
- One of the greatest challenges of Hajj is that, recently, there have been many accidents in Makkah due to the large numbers of Muslims attending. The possibility of being killed may put off some Muslims who wish to complete all of the Five Pillars but feel Hajj is too dangerous.

Other valid answers will be accepted.

90 Jihad

1 One mark will be awarded for each point identified up to a maximum of three marks. (3)
- Greater jihad is an inner struggle to be a better Muslim (1).
- Greater jihad involves Muslims resisting temptation in their daily lives (1).
- Muslims believe they can perform greater jihad by studying the Qur'an (1).
- Muslims believe they can perform greater jihad by helping people in their local community (1).
- Muslims believe they can perform greater jihad by attending the mosque regularly (1).

Other valid answers will be accepted.

2 One mark will be awarded for providing each way and a second mark for development of the way up to a maximum of four marks. (4)
- Jihad can be interpreted as greater jihad (1). This means that Muslims resist daily temptations in their lives (1).
- One aspect of greater jihad can be understood as helping others (1). The ummah is seen as important in Islam in supporting Muslims all over the world (1).
- Jihad can be understood as lesser jihad (1). This is understood as fighting in the name of Allah (1).

Other valid answers will be accepted.

91 Celebrations and commemorations

1 "Celebrating festivals such as Id-ul Adha is vital in Islam." Be sure to make your points specific, and refer to teachings and views, as you are instructed. You can support your arguments with Qur'anic or other teachings. Make sure you give balanced views and then draw a conclusion – make sure you say why this is your conclusion. In this question, 3 of the marks awarded will be for your spelling, punctuation and grammar, and your use of specialist terminology. (15)

Arguments for the statement:
- Id-ul Adha is significant today as it is still celebrated by Muslims at the end of Hajj. Id-ul Adha is the Festival of Sacrifice, signifying the completion of the Fifth Pillar of Islam, and it is celebrated with a special service, cards and gifts.
- Id-ul Adha continues to be significant today as it commemorates Ibrahim's willingness to sacrifice his son – a story from the Qur'an (Surah 37). This event shows how Ibrahim's faith was tested and Muslims believe they can learn from this and apply its meaning to their own lives.
- Festivals such as Id-ul Adha help to strengthen the ummah by uniting all Muslims. A key element of the festival is sacrificing and sharing an animal with the poor.

Arguments against the statement:
- Some Muslims may believe that celebrating Id-ul Adha is outdated as it recalls events that happened a long time ago. They may argue that the focus should be on the development of Islam in the world today rather than remembering the history of the religion.
- Some Muslims may recognise the celebration of Id-ul Adha as having some significance today, but also accept that other more practical celebrations in Islam can have a bigger impact in the world. Helping the poor – considered a duty – and giving money in Zakah, the Third Pillar of Islam, may have a bigger impact on uniting the ummah and caring for the poor than celebrating Id-ul Adha.
- Some Muslims may view festivals such as Id-ul Adha as materialistic and not what the religion of Islam is about. They may feel that the central part of Islam is being close to Allah, which can be achieved in other ways, such as praying regularly or attending the mosque with other Muslims.

Other valid answers will be accepted.

UNIT 4: MATTERS OF LIFE AND DEATH

92 Origins of the universe
1 One mark will be awarded for each point identified up to a maximum of three marks. (3)
   - Everything was created by Allah (1).
   - Balance was created in the universe (1).
   - Creation took periods of time (1).
   - Creation was planned by Allah (1).
   - Humans were created by Allah (1).
   Other valid answers will be accepted.
2 One mark will be awarded for providing each response and a second mark for development of the response up to a maximum of four marks. (4)
   - Some Muslims believe that science and Islam together explain how the universe was created (1). The 'Big Bang' explains how Allah created the universe (1).
   - Some Muslims do not see any conflict between Islam and scientific explanations (1). They believe that scientific explanations help them to understand Allah's creation (1).
   - Some Muslims view science and Islam as in conflict (1). The 'Big Bang' conflicts with the idea of Allah creating the universe (1).
   Other valid answers will be accepted.

93 Sanctity of life
1 One mark will be awarded for each point identified up to a maximum of three marks. (3)
   - All life was created by Allah (1).
   - Life should be respected (1).
   - All humans have equal worth (1).
   - Only Allah can take life away (1).
   - Life is sacred (1).
   Other valid answers will be accepted.
2 One mark will be awarded for providing each reason and a second mark for development of the reason up to a maximum of four marks. (4)
   - Muslims believe human life is holy because it was created by Allah (1). They believe it should be respected as it was made to be sacred (1).
   - Humans were given responsibilities directly from Allah, showing they are different from all other creations (1). Humans were made to be khalifahs or stewards for Allah (1).
   - Muslims believe human life is holy as the Qur'an contains teachings suggesting that the taking of life is wrong (1): 'whoever kills a soul … it is as if he had slain mankind entirely.' (Surah 5:32) (1)
   Other valid answers will be accepted.

94 The origins of human life
1 "It is possible to accept both evolution and Islamic ideas about the origin of human life." Be sure to make your points specific, and refer to teachings and views, as you are instructed. You can support your arguments with Qur'anic or other teachings. Make sure you give balanced views and then draw a conclusion – make sure you say why this is your conclusion. (12)
   Arguments for the statement:
   - Some Muslims argue that evolution was part of Allah's plan for creating humans and so bring Islamic ideas and science together. They believe that evolution explains how Allah created humans so that the strongest characteristics survived.
   - Many Muslims believe that science has more evidence and is more believable than earlier arguments about the origins of humans. They believe that although sources of authority such as the Qur'an are not wrong, they do need to adapt beliefs to the changing scientific world.
   - Many Muslims believe it is possible for science to offer a fuller explanation alongside Islam of how humans were

created by Allah. The two are not in conflict as science is able to develop Islamic beliefs about this topic and allows Muslims to understand better how human life was created.
   Arguments against the statement:
   - Qur'anic explanations of Allah's 'creation of man from clay' (Surah 32:7) appear to be in direct conflict with the theory of evolution, leaving no common ground between the two standpoints.
   - Some Muslims believe that there are too many differences between science and Islam and therefore reject all ideas that appear to conflict with traditional Islamic beliefs. Muslims want to believe that Allah planned and designed humans to be special, not that humans developed by adapting to their environments as the theory of evolution claims.
   - The Qur'an reinforces the view that Allah is the sole creator and designer of human life and that he did this without help, which contradicts scientific explanations. The Qur'an claims that Allah 'made from water every living thing.' (Surah 21:30)
   Other valid answers will be accepted.

95 Muslim attitudes to abortion
1 One mark will be awarded for providing each reason and a second mark for development of the reason up to a maximum of four marks. (4)
   - Some Muslims do not accept abortion as they believe in the sanctity of life (1). Life is regarded as sacred because it was created by Allah (1).
   - Some Muslims do not accept abortion as they believe it is against the Qur'an's teaching: 'And kill not your children for fear of poverty' (Surah 17:31) (1). Muslims believe only Allah can give and take life (1).
   - Some Muslims believe abortion is wrong because Allah gives each person a soul (1): 'the soul is breathed into his body.' (Sahih al-Bukhari 55:549) (1)
   Other valid answers will be accepted.
2 One mark will be awarded for providing each reason and a second mark for development of the reason up to a maximum of four marks. (4)
   - Some Muslims would respond by arguing that abortion is not acceptable due to the sanctity of life (1). Muslims believe life is sacred as it was created by Allah (1).
   - Some Muslims would respond by arguing that abortion is always wrong because the Qur'an teaches 'And kill not your children for fear of poverty' (Surah 17:31) (1). Muslims believe only Allah can give and take life (1).
   - Some Muslims may respond by arguing that there are some circumstances when abortion would be permitted if it protected the sanctity of the life of the mother (1), for example if the mother had been raped or if her health were put at risk (1).
   Other valid answers will be accepted.

96 Death and the afterlife (1)
1 One mark will be awarded for providing each reason and a second mark for development of the reason up to a maximum of four marks. (4)
   - The Qur'an contains many teachings stating that there is an afterlife (1). Surah 28 talks of the idea of resurrection (Surah 28:61) (1).
   - Muslims are taught that one of the characteristics of Allah is that he will judge them after death (1). Surah 39 says 'And to every soul will be paid in full (the fruit) of its Deeds.' (Surah 39:70) (1)
   - Muslims believe that having a reward or punishment in the afterlife seems fair and just (1). Islam teaches of the existence of paradise where the good will be rewarded and hell where people will be punished (1).
   Other valid answers will be accepted.
2 One mark will be awarded for providing each teaching and a second mark for development of the teaching up to a maximum of four marks. One further mark will be awarded for any relevant source of wisdom and authority. (5)

- The Qur'an talks of a 'Day of Resurrection' (Surah 28:61) (1). Islam teaches that on the Day of Resurrection Allah will judge humans on the way they have behaved during their lives on Earth (1): 'And to every soul will be paid in full (the fruit) of its Deeds.' (Surah 39:70) (1)
- There are many verses in the Qur'an which refer to Allah as a judge (1). Muslims believe Allah will decide whether a person deserves to be rewarded or punished in the afterlife (1): 'those who have believed … shall be made happy … and those who have rejected Faith … shall be brought forth to Punishment.' (Surah 30:15–16) (1)
- Muslims believe there is evidence in the Qur'an for a place of paradise for good people and a place of punishment for bad people (1): 'the Fire, which is prepared for the disbelievers.' (Surah 3:131) (1)

Other valid answers will be accepted.

97 Death and the afterlife (2)

1 "Everyone should believe in life after death." Be sure to make your points specific, and refer to teachings and views, as you are instructed. You can support your arguments with Qur'anic or other teachings. Make sure you give balanced views and then draw a conclusion – make sure you say why this is your conclusion. (12)

Arguments for the statement:
- A belief in life after death is important as it helps Muslims to understand how they should live their lives. Accepting the idea of reward or punishment after death means that they must know how Allah wants them to live in order to be rewarded in paradise (al-Jannah).
- There are many Muslim teachings on beliefs about life after death in sources of authority such as the Qur'an. Surah 28 talks of a 'Day of Resurrection' (Surah 28:61) when Allah will judge humans on the way they have behaved during their lives on Earth.
- Muslims believe that after death Allah will judge them on the Day of Judgement. This is important as belief in akhirah gives their lives meaning and purpose, and will impact on their behaviour and the way they treat others.

Arguments against the statement:
- Many non-religious people do not accept life after death as there is no proof. They think that belief in an afterlife gives a false sense of hope and there is no scientific evidence that it exists as no one has ever returned to prove it.
- Humanists believe there is no life after death: when a person dies their body just decays. They believe that life after death is impossible.
- Non-religious people claim that some people have been tricked into believing in an afterlife. They think that the promise of an afterlife was used in the past to control people's behaviour through the fear of punishment, but today reason tells us there is no afterlife.

Other valid answers will be accepted.

98 Euthanasia

1 One mark will be awarded for each point identified up to a maximum of three marks. (3)
- Allah created life and only he can take it away, which makes euthanasia wrong (1).
- The Qur'an teaches the sanctity of life as it is Allah's creation (1).
- The Qur'an teaches that only Allah can decide how long a person's life will be (1).
- Euthanasia is seen as suicide, which is not accepted in Islam (1).
- Suffering is regarded as an accepted test of faith in Islam (1).

Other valid answers will be accepted.

2 One mark will be awarded for providing each reason and a second mark for development of the reason up to a maximum of four marks. One further mark will be awarded for any relevant source of wisdom and authority. (5)

- Muslims do not accept euthanasia because they believe in the sanctity of life (1). The Qur'an teaches 'And do not kill yourselves (or one another)' (Surah 4:29) (1). This shows that life is special and sacred as it was created by Allah and, therefore, should not be ended by humans (1).
- Muslims believe euthanasia is wrong as all life is created by Allah (1). Muslims believe only Allah can decide when life begins and ends (1): 'Indeed we belong to Allah, and indeed to Him we will return.' (Surah 2:156) (1)
- Muslims do not accept euthanasia as the Qur'an teaches that it is seen as suicide (1). Islam teaches that ending your own life is against Allah (1): 'And no person can ever die except by Allah's Leave and at an appointed term.' (Surah 3:145) (1)
- Muslims believe euthanasia is wrong as Islam teaches that suffering has a purpose (1). Muslims believe that suffering may be a test of faith from Allah (1): 'Do the people think that they will be left to say, "We believe" and they will not be tried?' (Surah 29:2) (1)

Other valid answers will be accepted.

99 Issues in the natural world

1 "Muslims should protect animals." Be sure to make your points specific, and refer to teachings and views, as you are instructed. You can support your arguments with Qur'anic or other teachings. Make sure you give balanced views and then draw a conclusion – make sure you say why this is your conclusion. (12)

Arguments for the statement:
- Muslims may agree that animals should be protected as they believe the world is a gift Allah created for humans and should be respected. The Qur'an teaches: 'It is Allah who made for you the grazing animals upon which you ride, and some of them you eat' (Surah 40:79). This shows that although people can use animals and enjoy them, they are still Allah's creation.
- Muslims believe that they should protect animals because after death Allah will judge them on the way they have lived their lives. This includes the way they treated animals, so they should not mistreat or abuse them.
- Although Muslims believe the world was created by Allah, including the provision of animals as a gift to humanity, they also believe they were given the responsibility of being stewards (khalifahs). This means they believe that they should look after Allah's creation, including animals, and not exploit or abuse them.

Arguments against the statement:
- Many Muslims view humans as the ultimate part of Allah's creation. According to the sanctity of life argument, they were made to be special and different from animals, meaning that animals can be used by humans as they wish.
- Muslims may believe that Allah created animals for humans and therefore they do not need the protection of humans. Many Muslims are not vegetarian and eat meat, believing this is acceptable to Allah.
- Some Muslims may believe that as humans are superior to animals, animals can be used in experimentation if it will protect human life. Allah is believed to have given humans souls, making them sacred, whereas animals are not.

Other valid answers will be accepted.

UNIT 5: CRIME AND PUNISHMENT

100 Justice

1 "Justice is important for the victims of crime." Be sure to make your points specific, and refer to teachings and views, as you are instructed. You can support your arguments with Qur'anic or other teachings. Make sure you give balanced views and then draw a conclusion – make sure you say why this is your conclusion. (12)

Arguments for the statement:

- Islam teaches that justice is important for the victim. This is a key idea promoted in the Qur'an, which teaches Muslims to 'be persistently standing firm in justice' (Surah 4:135). This shows the importance of standing up for justice, including for that of the victim.
- Muslims believe that Islam is a religion based on justice because Allah himself is just. The Five Pillars teach Muslims to behave in a just way towards others. Providing justice for victims is in line with this idea and puts Muslim teachings into action.
- Muslims believe that after death they will be judged by Allah on the way they have lived their lives. Making sure that victims of crime receive justice is important in ensuring that everyone will be judged fairly on their actions after death.

Arguments against the statement:
- Some Muslims may believe that justice has a purpose wider than simply benefiting the victims of crime. Society in general, criminals and others who are possibly considering committing the same crime need to see that justice is being done and that there are consequences of crimes. This will help to maintain control in society.
- Many Muslims refer to Shari'ah law as their code of conduct when considering matters of justice. They would argue that following this law will provide justice for both the victim and also the offender – giving the criminal the opportunity to change and reform their behaviour.
- Muslims believe that equality is important and upholding justice can help to achieve this ideal. Although accepted for different reasons, in matters of crime all of those involved (victim, victim's family, offender and society) should be treated fairly and equally.

Other valid answers will be accepted.

101 Crime

1 One mark will be awarded for each point identified up to a maximum of three marks. (3)
- Islam teaches that crime is a distraction from Allah (1).
- Islam teaches that Allah knows all crimes committed (1).
- The Qur'an teaches that Allah orders justice (1).
- Islam teaches that criminals deserve to be treated fairly (1).
- Islam teaches that Muslims have a duty to help those who have committed crimes (1).

Other valid answers will be accepted.

2 One mark will be awarded for providing each way and a second mark for development of the way up to a maximum of four marks. (4)
- Organisations such as the Muslim Chaplains' Association work directly with prisoners (1). They support offenders after they are released and encourage them not to return to a life of crime (1).
- Organisations such as Mosaic operate a young offenders' programme (1). They educate young people about alternatives to a life of crime (1).
- Volunteers from the organisation Mosaic go into prisons to support young prisoners and to act as role models (1). They help them as they complete their prison sentences and look to rejoin society (1).

Other valid answers will be accepted.

102 Good, evil and suffering

1 One mark will be awarded for each point identified up to a maximum of three marks. (3)
- Islam teaches that Allah will reward Muslims who have followed his teachings in the afterlife (1).
- Muslims believe completing the Five Pillars of Islam will help them to achieve a reward in the afterlife (1).
- Islam teaches that helping others will help Muslims gain a reward in the afterlife (1).
- Islam teaches that the reward after death for good actions will be paradise for eternity (1).
- Islam teaches Muslims that Allah watches them and knows when they perform good actions (1).

Other valid answers will be accepted.
2 One mark will be awarded for providing each reason and a second mark for development of the reason up to a maximum of four marks. (4)
- Muslims believe that suffering has a purpose from Allah (1). It is part of his plan and therefore should not be questioned (1).
- Muslims believe that suffering may be a test of faith (1). It is a test of their commitment to Allah and the religion of Islam in the face of evil in the world (1).
- Islam teaches that suffering is a reminder of Muslims' daily struggle to overcome temptation and evil (1). Muslims believe that suffering is sometimes the result of human actions when they do wrong (1).

Other valid answers will be accepted.

103 Punishment

1 One mark will be awarded for providing each reason and a second mark for development of the reason up to a maximum of four marks. One further mark will be awarded for any relevant source of wisdom and authority. (5)
- Muslims believe that justice in the form of fair punishment is important when crimes have been committed (1). The Qur'an promotes the idea of justice through the concept of reward and punishment after death (1): 'But whoever transgresses after that will have a painful punishment.' (Surah 2:178) (1)
- Muslims also believe that the ummah requires stability in society, which can be achieved through just punishment when a crime has been committed (1). Both the Qur'an and Shari'ah law teach that Muslims should stand up for justice and fairness (1): 'O you who have believed, be persistently standing firm in justice, witnesses for Allah.' (Surah 4:135) (1)
- Just punishment gives offenders the opportunity to understand why their behaviour was wrong and to mend their ways (1). Allah is forgiving (1): 'Allah is Ever All-Knowing, All-Wise. He will admit to His Mercy whom He will.' (Surah 76:30–31)

Other valid answers will be accepted.

104 Aims of punishment

1 One mark will be awarded for each point identified up to a maximum of three marks. (3)
- There are specific instructions in the Qur'an for particular crimes (1).
- Punishment should be appropriate for the crime committed (1).
- Punishment should bring justice (1).
- Punishment should provide the chance to reform (1).
- Punishment should deter others from committing the same crime (1).

Other valid answers will be accepted.
2 One mark will be awarded for providing each reason and a second mark for development of the reason up to a maximum of four marks. (4)
- Muslims believe the Qur'an teaches that Allah is merciful and offenders should be given the opportunity to understand the difference between right and wrong (1). This will also help to provide stability to the ummah and to reinforce some of the other aims of punishment, such as protecting society (1).
- Muslims believe that forgiveness is important and that it gives criminals the chance to change their behaviour (1). Allah is believed to be just and forgiving, and Muslims believe that they should also develop these characteristics (1).
- Muslims believe that Allah will judge people after death on their actions, so giving offenders the chance to change their behaviour will allow them to become better Muslims (1). Helping and forgiving others also helps Muslims to achieve their goal of attaining al-Jannah (1).

Other valid answers will be accepted.

105 Forgiveness

1 "Criminals should always be forgiven." Be sure to make your points specific, and refer to teachings and views, as you are instructed. You can support your arguments with Qur'anic or other teachings. Make sure you give balanced views and then draw a conclusion – make sure you say why this is your conclusion. (12)

Arguments for the statement:
- The Qur'an teaches that Allah is merciful and forgiving, and Muslims believe that they should try to develop these characteristics in their own lives. Muslims should try to 'pardon and overlook, and forgive ...' (Surah 64:14).
- Islam is considered by Muslims to be a religion of peace and they believe they should work together to create a peaceful world. Putting this into practice means forgiving people when they do things that are wrong, and accepting that they are sorry in order to make peace with them.
- Muslims believe that after death they will be judged by Allah on the way they lived their lives. This includes showing forgiveness towards others and being sorry for wrongdoing in order to achieve a reward in al-Jannah with Allah.

Arguments against the statement:
- There may be some crimes it would be difficult to forgive. For example, if a member of a person's family was killed it might be difficult to forgive the offender, so some Muslims may feel that not all crimes can be forgiven.
- Fair justice is an important idea promoted in the Qur'an: 'be persistently standing firm in justice, witnesses for Allah' (Surah 4:135). However, in some cases of justice it may be hard to show forgiveness, especially where an offender may not be sorry for the crime they have committed.
- Some Muslims believe that Allah will judge them after death and that it is his place alone to be just and to forgive, especially in circumstances where violent crimes have been committed. They may believe that the law should punish criminals but that forgiveness should not necessarily be a part of this.

Other valid answers will be accepted.

106 Treatment of criminals

1 One mark will be awarded for each point identified up to a maximum of three marks. (3)
- Muslims believe criminals should be treated with justice (1).
- Muslims believe criminals should be treated humanely (1).
- Muslims believe criminals should be treated with respect (1).
- Muslims believe criminals should have basic human rights (1).
- Muslims believe criminals should not be tortured (1).

Other valid answers will be accepted.

2 One mark will be awarded for providing each reason and a second mark for development of the reason up to a maximum of four marks. (4)
- Muslims believe that all life – including that of prisoners – is sacred as it was created by Allah (1). The Qur'an teaches that all human life should be valued and respected, so prisoners should also have a right to life and recognition of their basic human rights (1).
- Muslims believe that because Allah is just, they should also act justly towards prisoners (1). The Qur'an teaches 'be persistently standing firm in justice' (Surah 4:135), so it is fair for prisoners to have basic human rights, e.g. food and water (1).
- Muslims believe that Allah will judge them after death on how they have behaved in life (1). Ensuring fair treatment of prisoners and recognising their basic human rights will help Muslims to achieve a reward in paradise (1).

Other valid answers will be accepted.

107 The death penalty

1 "Everyone should support the use of the death penalty." Be sure to make your points specific, and refer to teachings and views, as you are instructed. You can support your arguments with Qur'anic or other teachings. Make sure you give balanced views and then draw a conclusion – make sure you say why this is your conclusion. (12)

Arguments for the statement:
- There are teachings in Islam which suggest that the death penalty can be used for the crime of murder and for those who refuse to do their Islamic duty: 'in one of the three cases: the married adulterer, a life for life, and the deserter of his Din (Islam), abandoning the community ... [the death penalty is permissible].' (Sahih Muslim Hadith 16:4152)
- Some Muslims may point to the teachings of Muhammad which suggest that he agreed with the use of the death penalty, therefore making it acceptable for some crimes. For example, Hadith 682 talks of Muhammad ordering the death of a woman adulteress.
- Shari'ah law is used by Muslims to apply Islamic teachings and to decide punishments for crimes. It agrees with the teachings in the Qur'an, supporting the view that the death penalty can be used for some serious crimes.

Arguments against the statement:
- Many Muslims believe that although the Qur'an justifies the use of the death penalty for some crimes, it is not the only possible punishment. They may suggest that, in today's society, other punishments may be more appropriate for crimes, allowing criminals to reform and be forgiven.
- Muslims believe in the sanctity of life, which states that human life is special and sacred as it was created by Allah and given a soul: 'Then the soul is breathed into his body' (Sahih al-Bukhari 55:549). It is therefore wrong to take life, and so many Muslims would not support the use of the death penalty.
- Non-religious people such as Humanists would not support the use of the death penalty, believing that it is possible for errors to occur and that some innocent people could be put to death.

Other valid answers will be accepted.

UNIT 6: PEACE AND CONFLICT

108 Peace

1 One mark will be awarded for each point identified up to a maximum of three marks. (3)
- 'Islam' comes from the word 'salaam', often understood to mean 'peace' (1).
- Muslims greet each other with messages of peace (1).
- Muslims promote peace through standing up for justice (1).
- All Muslims are part of the ummah, which promotes equality and peace (1).
- The Qur'an talks of Muslims using 'words of peace' (Surah 25:63) (1).

Other valid answers will be accepted.

2 One mark will be awarded for providing each reason and a second mark for development of the reason up to a maximum of four marks. (4)
- The Qur'an teaches that Muslims should use 'words of peace' (Surah 25:63) (1). This shows that peace is important even when facing hatred or criticism from others (1).
- All Muslims are part of the ummah, which unites them in peace (1). Islam teaches Muslims that they have a duty from Allah to support and care for each other in peace (1).
- Muslims are taught to achieve justice in the world peacefully (1). Justice is a key idea taught in the Qur'an, with Muslims encouraged to remain 'standing firm in justice, witnesses for Allah.' (Surah 4:135) (1)

Other valid answers will be accepted.

109 Peacemaking

1 One mark will be awarded for providing each way and a second mark for development of the way up to a maximum of four marks. (4)

- The Muslim Peace Fellowship promotes ideas of peace in the world through education (1). It holds conferences and talks to demonstrate unity and peace between different religions (1).
- The Muslim Peace Fellowship reaches out to people of all faiths to work to reduce injustice in the world so that people can live in peace (1). It raises awareness of the situation of refugees and provides practical help to make society fairer and more peaceful (1).
- Islamic Relief provides emergency relief and aid in war-torn countries so peace can be restored (1). It provides medical care, food and water to relieve suffering and works to achieve peace between different groups (1).

Other valid answers will be accepted.

2 One mark will be awarded for providing each reason and a second mark for development of the reason up to a maximum of four marks. (4)
- Surah 41 talks of the importance of forgiveness and reconciliation in bringing peace to the world (Surah 41:34) (1). The Qur'an teaches that Allah created a world with the intention of people living together in peace (1).
- Islam teaches that Muslims have a duty to care for each other and to bring peace to the world (1). All Muslims are part of the ummah and are expected to look after and to support each other in peace (1).
- Many key teachings, beliefs and ideas in Islam are related to people living in peace with each other (1). The Five Pillars includes the concept of giving money in Zakah to help the poor and to create a fairer and more peaceful society (1).

Other valid answers will be accepted.

110 Conflict

1 One mark will be awarded for each point identified up to a maximum of three marks. (3)
- Muslims work to bring peace to groups in conflict (1).
- Muslims educate others to respect the equality of all as part of the ummah (1).
- Muslims work towards reconciliation through forgiveness (1).
- Some Muslims may fight as a last resort to restore peace (1).
- Some Muslims may fight to defend their religion (1).

Other valid answers will be accepted.

2 One mark will be awarded for providing each teaching and a second mark for development of the teaching up to a maximum of four marks. One further mark will be awarded for any relevant source of wisdom and authority. (5)
- The Qur'an teaches that it may be justified under certain conditions to fight in order to bring about the goal of peace, which is important to Muslims (1). Muslims recognise that fighting should be a last resort but that it can bring peace (1): 'And what is [the matter] with you that you fight not in the cause of Allah and [for] the oppressed among men, women, and children …' (Surah 4:75) (1).
- Islam teaches that any fighting that does happen should be fair and just (1). Muslims believe that Allah is just and that this should be applied to all situations, even war (1): 'Fight in the way of Allah those who fight you but do not transgress. Indeed, Allah does not like transgressors.' (Surah 2:190) (1)
- Islam teaches the importance of peace and forgiveness when faced with conflict (1). Muslims believe they should work to find peaceful solutions and to forgive others rather than fight (1): 'And the servants of the Most Merciful are those who walk upon the earth easily, and when the ignorant address them [harshly], they say [words of] peace.' (Surah 25:63) (1)

Other valid answers will be accepted.

111 Pacifism

1 "Muslims should all be pacifists." Be sure to make your points specific, and refer to teachings and views, as you are instructed. You can support your arguments with Qur'anic or other teachings. Make sure you give balanced views and then draw a conclusion – make sure you say why this is your conclusion. (12)

Arguments for the statement:
- Some Muslims may agree with this statement, believing that Islam is a religion of peace and that putting this into practice in the world can best be done through being pacifist. There are many teachings on peace in the Qur'an, showing that violence is not the answer.
- Some Muslims believe that they should be pacifists and work to achieve justice in the world because the Qur'an teaches that Allah created a world where people should live in peace together. This can only be achieved through peaceful means such as pacifism.
- The Qur'an stresses the importance of reconciliation and of working together to achieve unity – Surah 41 talks of justice, forgiveness and reconciliation helping to bring about peace. The ummah also demonstrates this as Muslims believe they have a duty to care and support all Muslims in the world and to work together for peace.

Arguments against the statement:
- Some Muslims may disagree with this statement as Islam is not traditionally associated with pacifism. Muhammad was forced to flee Makkah and there is evidence that he was forced to use violence, thus going against ideas of pacifism.
- Islam teaches in the Qur'an that sometimes violence is necessary in order to achieve peace, thus going against ideas of pacifism: 'Fight in the way of Allah those who fight you' (Surah 2:190). This recognises that there are cases where violence is sometimes justified in order to bring about peace.
- Warfare has been a part of Islam since the time of Muhammad, which goes against the principles of pacifism. Muhammad fought in the Battle of Badr and, more recently, the concept of lesser jihad has been used to justify the use of violence in defence of Islam.

Other valid answers will be accepted.

112 The Just War theory

1 One mark will be awarded for each point identified up to a maximum of three marks. (3)
- War should not target innocents (1).
- War should always be a last resort (1).
- War should only be fought when agreed by the whole community (1).
- War should not be fought to win land or power (1).
- War should always be an act of defence (1).

Other valid answers will be accepted.

2 One mark will be awarded for providing each way and a second mark for development of the way up to a maximum of four marks. (4)
- Some Muslims may recognise that war is sometimes necessary (1). They believe that the Just War theory considers war to be a last resort and supports the idea of protecting innocent life (1).
- Shi'a Muslims recognise lesser jihad (Just War) as one of the Ten Obligatory Acts (1). They believe the conditions of Just War theory ensure that war is fought for the right reasons and in the right way (1).
- Sunni Muslims do not place great emphasis on Just War theory (1). They may believe that reconciliation and forgiveness are at the heart of Islam and therefore believe that no war is justified (1).

Other valid answers will be accepted.

113 Holy war

1 One mark will be awarded for each point identified up to a maximum of three marks. (3)
- The Qur'an suggests that violence can be used if necessary (1).
- The Qur'an teaches the importance of peace and not war (Surah 8) (1).
- The Qur'an teaches that forgiveness should be shown if the opposition repents (Surah 9) (1).
- Holy war is justifiable in order to defend Islam (Surah 4) (1).

- The Qur'an suggests that Muslims should not attack others without good cause (Surah 2) (1).
Other valid answers will be accepted.
2 One mark will be awarded for providing each reason and a second mark for development of the reason up to a maximum of four marks. (4)
- The Qur'an teaches that violence can be used when it is considered necessary (Surah 9) (1). One of the conditions of holy war is that it be fought for the defence of Islam (1).
- One condition of holy war is to protect human life, which the Qur'an teaches is special (1). Muslims believe that human life is sacred as it was created by Allah (1).
- Holy war is accepted by Muslims if it is fought fairly and with justice (1). Muslims believe that Allah is just and fair, and the Qur'an encourages Muslims to act justly towards others, even in war (Surah 2) (1).
Other valid answers will be accepted.

114 Weapons of mass destruction

1 "Weapons of mass destruction should never be used." Be sure to make your points specific, and refer to teachings and views, as you are instructed. You can support your arguments with Qur'anic or other teachings. Make sure you give balanced views and then draw a conclusion – make sure you say why this is your conclusion. (12)
Arguments for the statement:
- Muslims believe that although the Qur'an doesn't say anything directly about the use of weapons of mass destruction (WMD), its teachings can be interpreted to show that they are wrong. The Qur'an suggests that if any person is killed, it would be like the killing of all mankind, showing that taking the life of others using WMD is wrong: 'whoever kills a soul … it is as if he had slain mankind entirely.' (Surah 5:32)
- Muslims support the sanctity of life theory, which is the idea that life is special and sacred as it is created by Allah. WMD threaten human life, causing the deaths of innocents, and their use therefore cannot be justified as it goes against this teaching.
- WMD cannot be justified due to the destruction they cause to the environment, which Muslims accept is the creation of Allah. The Qur'an teaches that Allah's creation should be respected and that humans are given the responsibility of being khalifahs, with a duty to care for the world. This would involve not supporting the use of WMD.
Arguments against the statement:
- Some people may support the use of WMD, using the ethical theory of utilitarianism as their justification. This ethical theory works on the principle of 'the greatest happiness for the greatest number' and the use of WMD could be justified if they are used as a deterrent to prevent war.
- Some people may support the use of WMD to bring about a quicker end to conflict. With traditional forms of warfare, each side could be evenly balanced in terms of conflict but with WMD one side might have an advantage and therefore a sustained and lengthy conflict could be prevented.
- Some people may support the use of WMD to minimise casualties on the side of those who use them. WMD give great power and advantage to the side that has them; they cause far more destruction and death than traditional methods of warfare.
Other valid answers will be accepted.

115 Issues surrounding conflict

1 One mark will be awarded for each point identified up to a maximum of three marks. (3)
- The Muslim Council of Britain runs education programmes. (1).
- Muslims can be involved in interfaith groups that work together to end conflict (1).
- Muslims can be involved in peaceful rallies to protest against conflict (1).

- Muslims can be part of organisations such as Mosaic, which works to reduce conflict (1).
- Muslims can take part in charity work to help those suffering as a result of conflict (1).
Other valid answers will be accepted.
2 One mark will be awarded for providing each way and a second mark for development of the way up to a maximum of four marks. (4)
- Some Muslims may be involved in charity work to help those suffering as a result of conflict (1). They could be part of an organisation such as Islamic Relief, which works to bring aid to people in places of conflict (1).
- Some Muslims may speak out against those who commit atrocities in the world (1), for example the Muslim Council of Britain has spoken out after Islamic extremist attacks (1)
- Some Muslims may work to educate people about the peaceful messages Islam promotes (1). They could become involved in an interfaith group that helps to find common ground between religions and works to bring an end to conflict (1).
Other valid answers will be accepted.

UNIT 7: PHILOSOPHY OF RELIGION

116 Revelation

1 One mark will be awarded for each point identified up to a maximum of three marks. (3)
- Allah chooses to reveal himself directly through the Qur'an (1).
- Muslims believe that they can understand what Allah is like through the Qur'an (1).
- Muslims believe the Qur'an is proof of Allah's existence (1)
- Muslims believe the Qur'an reveals how Allah wants them to live their lives (1).
- Muslims believe the Qur'an reveals Allah is omnipotent (1).
Other valid answers will be accepted.
2 One mark will be awarded for each point identified up to a maximum of three marks. (3)
- The Qur'an shows that Allah is omnipotent (1).
- The Qur'an shows that Allah is omniscient (1).
- The Qur'an shows that Allah is benevolent (1).
- The Qur'an shows that Allah is transcendent (1).
- The Qur'an shows that Allah is immanent (1).
Other valid answers will be accepted.

117 Visions

1 One mark will be awarded for providing each reason and a second mark for development of the reason up to a maximum of four marks. (4)
- Visions show Muslims that Allah is all-powerful and are proof that he exists (1). For example, Allah spoke to Musa in a vision in order to communicate with humanity (1).
- Muslims believe that Allah's nature is revealed in visions such as the one Mary received (1). The Qur'anic account reveals that Allah is merciful and chose Mary to be the mother of Isa (Surah 19:16–20) (1).
- Many Muslims believe that Allah is transcendent and cannot therefore be seen directly, so visions help to connect him to humanity (1). This can be seen in the example of Moses (Surah 7) (1).
Other valid answers will be accepted.
2 One mark will be awarded for providing each reason and a second mark for development of the reason up to a maximum of four marks. (4)
- Some Muslims prefer to look to other sources of revelation that they feel offer stronger proof of Allah's existence (1). The Qur'an is a direct source of revelation from Allah and tells Muslims about the nature of Allah, as well as being proof of his existence (1).
- Some Muslims believe that having faith in Allah means having trust without proof (1). Shi'a Muslims hold this point of view (1).

- Some Muslims believe that Allah is transcendent and too great to be fully understood through visions (1). For example, in the Qur'an the vision experienced by Musa was not a direct vision of Allah (1).

Other valid answers will be accepted.

118 Miracles

1 "Miracles are evidence of Allah's existence." Be sure to make your points specific, and refer to teachings and views, as you are instructed. You can support your arguments with Qur'anic or other teachings. Make sure you give balanced views and then draw a conclusion – make sure you say why this is your conclusion. (12)

Arguments for the statement:
- The Qur'an is a source of authority for Muslims because it is given to them by Allah; including miracles in the Qur'an gives them significance. Examples of miracles such as Nuh and the flood help to strengthen the argument that Allah exists.
- Muslims believe that miracles demonstrate the nature of Allah and, in turn, prove that he exists. Miracles demonstrate Allah's power over and love for the world. They allow him to connect with humanity in order to reveal what he is like and to confirm his existence.
- Many Muslims believe that miracles allow them to understand Allah better and to become closer to him. Miracles are evidence of Allah working within the world and examples such as Al-Mi'raj – where Muhammad was taken to meet Allah – reinforce the fact that he exists.

Arguments against the statement:
- Some Muslims do not place great emphasis on miracles as proof of the existence of Allah. Instead, they may see the example of Muhammad as a prophet or the Qur'an itself as more significant sources of authority in strengthening their view that Allah exists.
- Non-religious people might offer alternative explanations for miracles, thereby challenging whether they prove the existence of Allah. They might use science to show that miracles do not happen, and that events considered to be miraculous may have reasonable explanations that need no reference to Allah.
- Some Muslims may accept that miracles happen, but believe they are not necessary in order to have faith and belief in Allah. They may believe that having faith in Allah means trusting that he exists without needing further proof of this.

Other valid answers will be accepted.

119 Religious experiences

1 One mark will be awarded for each point identified up to a maximum of three marks. (3)
- Muslims believe that religious experiences reveal the nature of Allah (1).
- Muslims believe that religious experiences can take the form of visions (1).
- Muslims believe that religious experiences can take the form of miracles (1).
- Muslims believe that the Qur'an was revealed to Muhammad through a religious experience (1).
- Muslims believe that they can gain a personal understanding of Allah through religious experiences (1).

Other valid answers will be accepted.

2 One mark will be awarded for providing each reason and a second mark for development of the reason up to a maximum of four marks. (4)
- Religious experiences reveal the nature of Allah. Muslims believe that Allah's power is shown by revealing himself to prophets such as Muhammad (1). For example, visions and miracles show the power Allah has (1).
- Religious experiences strengthen faith in Allah (1), for example Muhammad's religious experiences confirm that Allah wants to connect with humanity (1).

- Prophet Muhammad received the Qur'an through a religious experience (1). This final perfect message from Allah began the religion of Islam (1).

Other valid answers will be accepted.

120 The design argument

1 One mark will be awarded for each point identified up to a maximum of three marks. (3)
- The design argument shows that Allah is omnipotent (1).
- The design argument shows that Allah is benevolent (1).
- The design argument shows that Allah is omniscient (1).
- The design argument shows that Allah is the designer of the universe (1).
- The design argument shows that Allah is transcendent (1).

Other valid answers will be accepted.

2 One mark will be awarded for providing each way and a second mark for development of the way up to a maximum of four marks. (4)
- Muslims will argue for the design argument, suggesting that Allah is the only good explanation for the design perceived within the world (1). The Qur'an gives the examples of rain, wind and clouds as evidence of the design in the world attributed to Allah (Surah 2) (1).
- Muslims may argue that evolution was part of Allah's design for the world (1). They believe scientific criticisms that try to damage the view that Allah designed the world can be used as part of the Islamic explanation to strengthen their argument (1).
- Muslims may argue that bad design in the world does not disprove the design argument (1). Bad design may have a purpose that humans are not yet aware of (1).

Other valid answers will be accepted.

121 The cosmological argument

1 One mark will be awarded for providing each characteristic and a second mark for development of the characteristic up to a maximum of four marks. (4)
- The cosmological argument reveals that Allah is omnipotent (1). He is shown to have the power to create everything within the universe, including humans (1).
- The cosmological argument reveals that Allah is benevolent (1). He cares for his creation and created everything humans needed, including food, water and shelter (1).
- The cosmological argument reveals that Allah is omniscient (1). He was able to see what he created and did it in such a way that it all worked together (1).

Other valid answers will be accepted.

2 One mark will be awarded for providing each reason and a second mark for development of the reason up to a maximum of four marks. (4)
- Muslims believe the cosmological argument proves that there is a creator of the universe – Allah (1). Muslims accept that only Allah, who is omnipotent, could have created the universe (1).
- Muslims believe that the cosmological argument reinforces teachings in the Qur'an (1). Surah 79:27 says, referring to the universe, 'Are you more difficult to create, or is the heaven that He constructed?' (1).
- Muslims believe the cosmological argument proves that the universe has a creator who is benevolent towards his creation (1). Al-Ghazali put forward the 'kalam' version of the cosmological argument, which stated that there must be a cause of the universe (1).

Other valid answers will be accepted.

122 The existence of suffering

1 One mark will be awarded for each point identified up to a maximum of three marks. (3)
- The existence of suffering challenges whether Allah exists (1).
- The existence of suffering questions whether Allah is omnipotent (1).

- The existence of suffering questions whether Allah loves his creation (1).
- The existence of suffering questions whether Allah is omniscient (1).
- The existence of suffering questions whether Allah is just (1).
Other valid answers will be accepted.

2 One mark will be awarded for providing each reason and a second mark for development of the reason up to a maximum of four marks. (4)
- Suffering challenges the power of Allah (1). Muslims may question why Allah doesn't prevent the excessive amount of suffering that people face if he is able to do something about it (1).
- Suffering calls into question whether Allah is all-loving (1). The Qur'an says 'In the Name of Allah, the Most Beneficent, the Most Merciful …' (Surah 1:1), which suggests his benevolence, but this is challenged by the presence of suffering in the world (1).
- The existence of suffering calls into question whether Allah is omniscient (1). Muslims might question why Allah does nothing to help those who suffer if he knows everything that happens in the world (1).
Other valid answers will be accepted.

123 Solutions to the problem of suffering

1 One mark will be awarded for providing each way and a second mark for development of the way up to a maximum of four marks. (4)
- Muslims may respond by joining a charity that works to help those who are suffering (1). For example, they could volunteer for or make a donation to Muslim Aid, which responds to disasters (1).
- Muslims may pray more often for those who are suffering (1). Muslims believe Allah will listen to their prayers and help those who are suffering by giving them the strength to cope (1).
- Muslims could read the Qur'an and share its message about suffering with those who are affected (1). Teachings that tell Muslims to 'seek help through patience and prayer' (Surah 2:153) may encourage them not to give up (1).
Other valid answers will be accepted.

2 One mark will be awarded for providing each teaching and a second mark for development of the teaching up to a maximum of four marks. One further mark will be awarded for any relevant source of wisdom and authority. (5)
- The Qur'an teaches Muslims to turn to prayer to cope with suffering (1). Muslims believe they should put their faith in Allah and pray for the strength to cope with suffering (1): 'O you who have believed, seek help through patience and prayer. Indeed, Allah is with the patient.' (Surah 2:153) (1)
- The Qur'an teaches Muslims that suffering is a test of their faith from Allah (1). They believe they should not question why they suffer, but instead accept that it has a higher purpose (1): 'And We will surely test you with something of fear and hunger and a loss of wealth and lives and fruits, but give glad tidings to the patient, Who, when disaster strikes them, say, "Indeed we belong to Allah, and indeed to Him we will return." ' (Surah 2:155–156) (1)
- Muslims believe they should use the presence of suffering in the world to develop positive characteristics like Allah by praying for strength (1). Muslims believe suffering helps them to appreciate the good in the world and makes them stronger (1): 'O you who have believed, seek help through patience and prayer. Indeed, Allah is with the patient.' (Surah 2:153) (1)
Other valid answers will be accepted.

UNIT 8: EQUALITY

124 Human rights

1 "Muslims should always support human rights." Be sure to make your points specific, and refer to teachings and views, as you are instructed. You can support your arguments with Qur'anic or other teachings. Make sure you give balanced views and then draw a conclusion – make sure you say why this is your conclusion. (12)
Arguments for the statement:
- Many Muslims believe that standing up for the rights of others is a duty given to them by Allah. They believe that Allah created all humans to be equal, an idea that is reinforced in the Qur'an: 'And of His signs is the creation of the heavens and the earth, and the difference of your languages and colours' (Surah 30:22). This recognises that differences between people do not matter and all people are equal. Muslims believe that they should help to ensure equality is attained for all humans.
- There are examples of Muhammad standing up for the rights of others – particularly women and children. Muslims believe they should follow the example of Muhammad, as he was the prophet chosen by Allah to guide them.
- The Qur'an includes teachings that are seen to support human rights and to ensure justice is attained: 'O you who have believed, be persistently standing firm for Allah, witnesses in justice, and do not let the hatred of a people prevent you from being just' (Surah 5:8). Muslims believe that Allah is just and so they should also try to be just.
Arguments against the statement:
- Some Muslims may believe that although human rights are important, it may be acceptable to deny people certain rights in some circumstances. For example, if a person's freedom has been taken away from them as punishment for a crime, they should accept this.
- Some human rights – for example, same-sex marriage – may conflict with traditional Islamic beliefs. As some Muslims do not accept same-sex marriage due to Islamic teachings, they would not find it possible to stand up for these human rights.
- Muslims may believe that standing up for human rights is sometimes not the right action to take, for example in cases where they may come into conflict with the laws of the country in which they live. They may believe that only those in authority should get involved in such cases.
Other valid answers will be accepted.

125 Equality

1 One mark will be awarded for each point identified up to a maximum of three marks. (3)
- All Muslims pray at the same time (1).
- All Muslims complete the Five Pillars (1).
- All Muslims wear white on Hajj (1).
- All Muslims fast during Ramadan (1).
- All Muslims donate money in Zakah (1).
Other valid answers will be accepted.

2 One mark will be awarded for providing each reason and a second mark for development of the reason up to a maximum of four marks. (4)
- Islam teaches that humans were created equal by Allah and Muslims have a duty to work to achieve this (1). Muslims believe that they should stand up and help those who are not treated equally, such as those living in poverty (1).
- Muslims believe that as Allah is just they should also be just and work towards equal treatment of others (1). Muslims should 'be persistently standing firm in justice, witnesses for Allah' (Surah 4:135), suggesting that they should stand up for justice and equality for those who do not have it (1).
- Practices in Islam such as donating money in Zakah, which is a duty, demonstrate how all Muslims are expected to work towards equality (1). Sharing money through annual

charitable donations helps to address financial inequality in the world (1).

Other valid answers will be accepted.

126 Religious freedom

1 "Religious freedom is important in a multifaith society." Be sure to make your points specific, and refer to teachings and views, as you are instructed. You can support your arguments with Qur'anic or other teachings. Make sure you give balanced views and then draw a conclusion – make sure you say why this is your conclusion. (12)

Arguments for the statement:

- Some Muslims believe that religious freedom is important because of the many benefits it brings to society. It allows different groups to interact and share their faiths, leading to greater understanding. It also gives Muslims the opportunity to connect with people from other faiths in interfaith networks in order to work towards greater justice and equality in society.
- Some Muslims believe that although Islam is the true faith and the final message from Allah, other faiths also contain important elements of truth that should be respected. Islam recognises many prophets from the religions of Christianity and Judaism, for example Abraham, Noah and Moses.
- Some Muslims believe that as long as a person is righteous, they will be favoured by Allah, regardless of their religion. This shows that all faiths are equally valid and Muslims accept that there are many ways to achieve their goal of paradise after death.

Arguments against the statement:

- Some Muslims do not accept religious freedom, as they believe that Islam is the only true faith and that Muslims have a duty to introduce Islam to non-Muslims. They believe other faiths do not convey the complete truth and that only Islam contains the final correct message from Allah.
- Some non-religious people may feel that complete religious freedom is wrong and that some faith practices should not be accepted in an increasingly atheist society. They may object to the practices of some religions, for example the way animals are killed for halal meat in Islam or the idea that Friday is a holy day.
- Some Muslims may believe that although it is an important goal, there is too much opposition to religious freedom and tolerance in today's society for it to be overcome. Muslims may feel that they increasingly face unfair discrimination or intolerance as a result of terrorist acts by minority extremist groups.

Other valid answers will be accepted.

127 Prejudice and discrimination

1 One mark will be awarded for providing each reason and a second mark for development of the reason up to a maximum of four marks. One further mark will be awarded for any relevant source of wisdom and authority. (5)

- Muslims believe that prejudice and discrimination go against teachings, such as those found in the Qur'an, that Allah created all people as equal but different (1): 'We have created you from male and female and made you peoples and tribes that you may know one another.' (Surah 49:13) (1)
- Muslims follow the teachings of Muhammad, who emphasised the importance of treating all people as equal in his final sermon (1): 'All mankind is descended from Adam and Eve' (Muhammad). This shows there is no difference between humans and that they should be treated equally (1).
- Muslims believe that it is important to be tolerant of other religions and to educate others about religion rather than discriminating against them if they are of a different faith (1). Many Muslims work as members of interfaith groups to challenge inequality in the world (1).

Other valid answers will be accepted.

128 Racial harmony

1 Award one mark for each point identified up to a maximum of three. (3)

- All mankind is descended from Adam and Eve (1).
- All humans are created equal by Allah (1).
- All Muslims are equal in the ummah (1).
- Muhammad taught that there is no difference between people from different races (1).
- The Qur'an teaches that all races are equally valid (1).

Other valid answers will be accepted.

2 One mark will be awarded for providing each reason and a second mark for development of the reason up to a maximum of four marks. (4)

- Muslims believe that all humans from all races were created equal by Allah to live in peace together (1). This is reinforced in the Qur'an: 'We have created you from male and female and made you peoples and tribes that you may know one another.' (Surah 49:13) (1)
- Muhammad taught about the importance of racial harmony in his last sermon (1): 'an Arab is not better than a non-Arab and a non-Arab is not better than an Arab' (Muhammad). This shows that all people are of equal value and should be treated the same (1).
- Muslims are all part of the greater Islamic community – the ummah – and are all considered equal regardless of race (1). Islamic practices such as following the Five Pillars reflect this, as all Muslims perform the same actions wherever they happen to be (1).

Other valid answers will be accepted.

129 Racial discrimination

1 One mark will be awarded for each point identified up to a maximum of three marks. (3)

- Racial discrimination is wrong because Allah created all humans equal (1).
- Muhammad taught that all humans are descended from Adam and Eve and are equal (1).
- The Qur'an recognises both diversity and equal value among people (1).
- Muhammad taught that there is no difference between people of different races (1).
- Muslims of all races are considered equal in the ummah (1).

Other valid answers will be accepted.

2 One mark will be awarded for providing each reason and a second mark for development of the reason up to a maximum of four marks. (4)

- Muslims believe that all people are descended from Adam and Eve and so deserve to be treated the same (1). Racial discrimination can lead to races being attacked, which is wrong (1).
- Muhammad taught in his last sermon that all races were equal (1). Racial discrimination can lead to races being targeted and misunderstood (1).
- The Qur'an teaches that while there is diversity between people, all races are still equal (Surah 30:22) (1). This idea is reflected in the Muslim idea of the ummah, which promotes unity rather than difference as all Muslims perform the same acts regardless of race (1).

Other valid answers will be accepted.

130 Social justice

1 One mark will be awarded for each point identified up to a maximum of three marks. (3)

- The Qur'an teaches Muslims to help each other (1).
- Muslims believe they will be judged after death on how they contributed to social justice (1).
- Islam teaches that everyone is human and deserves human rights (1).
- Shari'ah law promotes ideas of social justice (1).
- The Five Pillars promote ideas of social justice (1).

Other valid answers will be accepted.

2　One mark will be awarded for providing each reason and a second mark for development of the reason up to a maximum of four marks. (4)
- Allah is considered to be just and Muslims believe they should also behave with justice towards others (1). Muslims believe that Allah will judge them after death on how they have behaved (1).
- The Qur'an talks of the duty that Muslims have to work for social justice by helping others: 'So they who have believed in him, honoured him, supported him and followed the light which was sent down with him – it is those who will be the successful' (Surah 7:157) (1). Muslims believe that working for social justice will create more equality in the world (1).
- Muslims must give Zakah every year, which is one of the Five Pillars (1). Zakah money is usually given to charities and is used to help the poor in society and to tackle issues of social injustice (1).
Other valid answers will be accepted.

131 Wealth and poverty

1　"All Muslims should share their wealth with others." Be sure to make your points specific, and refer to teachings and views, as you are instructed. You can support your arguments with Qur'anic or other teachings. Make sure you give balanced views and then draw a conclusion – make sure you say why this is your conclusion. (12)

Arguments for the statement:
- Muslims are taught to share their wealth with others through charity. Zakah is one of the Five Pillars and it is a duty in Islam for Muslims to donate 2.5 per cent of their income annually. Muslims do this to support the poor and to reduce poverty, which is a key teaching in the Qur'an: '[true] righteousness is [in] one who … gives zakah.' (Surah 2:177)
- Muslims are taught that wealth is a gift from Allah and should be used honestly to help others: 'be steadfast in prayer and regular in charity' (Surah 2:110). Many Muslims voluntarily support charities such as Islamic Relief or Muslim Aid.
- Muslims believe that they will be judged after death on how they have acted towards others during their lives. Sharing their money with others is believed to please Allah and will help them to achieve their goal of paradise.

Arguments against the statement:
- Some Muslims may believe that although wealth is not ultimately the most important thing in life, it is a gift from Allah and therefore not a bad thing.
- Some Muslims may believe that they can offer more practical help to others instead of giving money. They may think that volunteering with a charity can bring greater benefits to those in need.
- Some Muslims may believe that it is not always possible to share wealth with others, such as in cases where people may not be able to afford to give Zakah.
Other valid answers will be accepted.

132 (a) type questions

1　One mark will be awarded for each point identified up to a maximum of three marks. (3)
- One of the Six Beliefs is Tawhid (1).
- One of the Six Beliefs is a belief in angels (1).
- One of the Six Beliefs is the authority of holy books (1).
- One of the Six Beliefs is acceptance of the prophets (1).
- One of the Six Beliefs is a belief in life after death (1).
Other valid answers will be accepted.

2　One mark will be awarded for each point identified up to a maximum of three marks. (3)
- The Qur'an was revealed to Muhammad (1).
- The Qur'an was revealed over 23 years (1).
- The Qur'an came directly from Allah (1).

- The Qur'an helps guide Muslims (1).
- The Qur'an tells Muslims how Allah wants them to live their lives (1).
Other valid answers will be accepted.

3　One mark will be awarded for each point identified up to a maximum of three marks. (3)
- Muslims will want to follow the laws of Allah (1).
- Muslims will try to live good lives in order to be rewarded in the afterlife (1).
- Muslims will constantly be aware of their thoughts, beliefs and actions (1).
- Muslims will try to help others as this is what Allah wants (1).
- Muslims will try to perform the Five Pillars for Allah (1).
Other valid answers will be accepted.

4　One mark will be awarded for each point identified up to a maximum of three marks. (3)
- Muslims believe that sex is an act of worship (1).
- Muslims believe that the purpose of sex is procreation (1).
- Muslims believe that sex fulfils physical, emotional and spiritual needs (1).
- Muslims believe that sex should only take place within marriage (1).
- Adultery is forbidden in Islam (1).
Other valid answers will be accepted.

5　One mark will be awarded for each point identified up to a maximum of three marks. (3)
- Divorce is allowed in Islam as a last resort (1).
- Divorce is hated by Allah (1).
- The Qur'an contains guidelines on divorce (1).
- A couple are expected to try to reconcile before considering divorce (1).
- A Muslim man can divorce a woman (1).
Other valid answers will be accepted.

6　One mark will be awarded for each point identified up to a maximum of three marks. (3)
- The Shahadah is recited in public (1).
- The Shahadah is spoken before death (1).
- The Shahadah is whispered into the ears of newborn babies (1).
- The Shahadah is part of the adhan (1).
- The Shahadah is recited daily by Muslims (1).
Other valid answers will be accepted.

7　One mark will be awarded for each point identified up to a maximum of three marks. (3)
- Khums is given by Shi'a Muslims (1).
- Khums is 20 per cent of extra income (1).
- The descendants of Muhammad receive khums (1).
- Khums can be used to build Islamic schools (1).
- Khums can be used to help the poor and needy (1).
Other valid answers will be accepted.

8　One mark will be awarded for each point identified up to a maximum of three marks. (3)
- During Id-ul Fitr homes will be decorated (1).
- During Id-ul Fitr special mosque services will be held (1).
- During Id-ul Fitr Id cards will be sent to friends and family (1).
- During Id-ul Fitr a celebratory meal will be shared (1).
- During Id-ul Fitr extra prayers will be said to thank Allah (1).
Other valid answers will be accepted.

9　One mark will be awarded for each point identified up to a maximum of three marks. (3)
- Muslims believe that human life was created by Allah (1).
- The Qur'an says it is wrong to take away life (1).
- Muslims believe that human life is a gift from Allah (1).
- Muslims believe that humans have a soul (1).
- Islam teaches that only Allah can give and take away life (1).
Other valid answers will be accepted.

10 One mark will be awarded for each point identified up to a maximum of three marks. (3)
- Muslims can care for animals (1).
- Muslims can recycle items (1).
- Muslims can try to reduce pollution (1).
- Muslims can plant trees (1).
- Muslims can campaign to care for Allah's creation (1).
Other valid answers will be accepted.

11 One mark will be awarded for each point identified up to a maximum of three marks. (3)
- Justice is a key idea promoted in the Qur'an (1).
- Shari'ah law has strict rules on justice (1).
- The Five Pillars demonstrate ideas of justice (1).
- Muslims believe that Allah is just (1).
- Islam teaches that Muslims should stand up for justice (1).
Other valid answers will be accepted.

12 One mark will be awarded for each point identified up to a maximum of three marks. (3)
- Islam teaches that punishment can be a form of justice (1).
- Islam teaches that punishment can contribute to a peaceful society (1).
- Islam teaches that punishment allows criminals to change their behaviour (1).
- Islam teaches that punishment is needed to maintain law and order (1).
- Islam teaches that punishment helps to keep society safe (1).
Other valid answers will be accepted.

13 One mark will be awarded for each point identified up to a maximum of three marks. (3)
- Muslims can support Islamic Relief (1).
- Muslims can forgive those who do wrong to them (1).
- Muslims can campaign for people to work together (1).
- Muslims can work with different faiths for peace (1).
- Muslims can pray (1).
Other valid answers will be accepted.

14 One mark will be awarded for each point identified up to a maximum of three marks. (3)
- Visions help Muslims get closer to Allah (1).
- Visions show that Allah is omnipotent (1).
- Muhammad received visions (1).
- Visions are a way for Allah to communicate with humanity (1).
- Musa received a vision from Allah (1).
Other valid answers will be accepted.

15 One mark will be awarded for each point identified up to a maximum of three marks. (3)
- Muslims may pray (1).
- Muslims may donate money (1).
- Muslims may support Muslim Aid (1).
- Muslims may believe that suffering is part of a test in life (1).
- Muslims may read the Qur'an (1).
Other valid answers will be accepted.

16 One mark will be awarded for each point identified up to a maximum of three marks. (3)
- The Qur'an teaches that all mankind is descended from Adam and Eve (1).
- Islam demonstrates racial harmony through the ummah (1).
- Muhammad declared in his final sermon that there was no difference between Arabs and non-Arabs (1).
- The Qur'an teaches that no race is better than any other (1).
- Islam teaches that Allah created all humans to live together peacefully (1).
Other valid answers will be accepted.

133 (b) type questions
1 One mark will be awarded for providing each root and a second mark for development of the root up to a maximum of four marks. (4)
- One of the five roots of 'Usul ad-Din is Tawhid (1). Muslims believe in one God who is called Allah (1).
- One of the five roots of 'Usul ad-Din is Adl (1). This is divine justice as Allah is understood to be fair and just in his treatment of everything (1).
- One of the five roots of 'Usul ad-Din is Nubuwwah (1). This is prophethood and the belief that Allah appointed messengers to communicate with humanity (1).
Other valid answers will be accepted.

2 One mark will be awarded for providing each belief and a second mark for development of the belief up to a maximum of four marks. (4)
- Prophets are messengers from Allah (1). Muslims believe that Allah communicated with prophets such as Ibrahim in order to give important messages to humanity such as how to worship (1).
- Prophets are seen as role models for Muslims (1). For example, Ishma'il is praised for being patient and kind – characteristics that Muslims are expected to demonstrate (1).
- Prophets are believed to bring the words of Allah to humanity (1). Muhammad was given the Qur'an, which is the words of Allah (1).
Other valid answers will be accepted.

3 One mark will be awarded for describing each Muslim belief and a second mark for each contrasting Christian belief up to a maximum of four marks. (4)
- Islam teaches that individual sinners must ask for forgiveness before death in order to be forgiven (1). Christians believe that the sacrifice of Jesus atoned for the sins of the world (1).
- Islam accepts the idea of barzakh, which is the stage between death and a judgement from Allah (1). Christians accept the idea of purgatory, which is a waiting place following judgement where they go before their souls are cleansed in preparation for heaven (1).
- Muslims believe in angels who record the good and bad deeds of each individual Muslim (1). Christians do not believe that angels record the good and bad deeds of individual Christians (1).
Other valid answers will be accepted.

4 One mark will be awarded for providing each reason and a second mark for development of the reason up to a maximum of four marks. (4)
- Life after death is a key teaching in the Qur'an (1). Muslims believe Surah 17:71 talks of a Day of Judgement where Muslims will be judged (1).
- Muslims are taught that Allah will judge them after death (1). Muslims believe life is a test and that everything they do and think is recorded by angels for judgement in the afterlife (1).
- The Qur'an describes heaven and hell in detail (1). Heaven is a place of paradise and a reward, while hell is a place of torment and punishment (1).
Other valid answers will be accepted.

5 One mark will be awarded for providing each teaching and a second mark for development of the teaching up to a maximum of four marks. (4)
- Muslim parents are understood to have the responsibility of raising their children correctly (1). They are expected to introduce their children to the Islamic faith (1).
- The family is seen as the foundation of the ummah (1). It gives stability to society and is the basic unit of support for Muslims (1).
- The family is understood by Muslims to provide a loving and caring atmosphere in which to have children (1). Muslims believe they have a duty to marry and procreate in order to contribute to the religion of Islam (1).
Other valid answers will be accepted.

6 One mark will be awarded for providing each way and a second mark for development of the way up to a maximum of four marks. (4)
- The family can be supported through prayer (1). Muslim families attend the mosque together to show children how to worship Allah (1).

- Parents can attend classes to support and help them in their parental role (1). In these classes, help and advice can be given to support parents in raising their children correctly according to Islam (1).
- Families can celebrate important rites of passage together and within the Muslim community (1). Births, marriages and funerals help to bring people together and to celebrate the gifts Allah has given (1).

Other valid answers will be accepted.

7   One mark will be awarded for providing each teaching and a second mark for development of the teaching up to a maximum of four marks. (4)
- Gender prejudice and discrimination is wrong as Islam teaches that everyone is Allah's creation (1). Although men and women were not created to be the same, Muslims are taught that they were created to be of equal worth (1).
- Islam teaches that men and women will be judged in the same way after death (1). Men and women should not be treated differently as all are equal before Allah when they have to account for their actions on Earth (1).
- Men and women are understood to have the same rights in terms of Islam and pleasing Allah (1). Islam gives men and women equal responsibility to marry, have a family and care for Allah's creation (1).

Other valid answers will be accepted.

8   One mark will be awarded for providing each purpose and a second mark for development of the purpose up to a maximum of four marks. (4)
- The Ten Obligatory Acts are duties all Shi'a Muslims should perform (1). They help to guide Muslims in how they should live their lives (1).
- The Ten Obligatory Acts offer ways of getting closer to Allah (1). They are all actions – for example, prayer – which Allah expects Muslims to perform (1).
- The Ten Obligatory Acts help Muslims to achieve their goal of paradise in the afterlife (1). Islam teaches that through performing Sawm, giving Zakah and following the other acts Muslims will please Allah and be rewarded with heaven when they die (1).

Other valid answers will be accepted.

9   One mark will be awarded for providing each condition and a second mark for development of the condition up to a maximum of four marks. (4)
- One condition is that there has to be a just cause for lesser jihad (1). It should be fought to protect or defend Islam (1).
- One condition is that it should be fought as a last resort (1). All other ways of trying to resolve the conflict – for example, talking and working together – should have been tried first (1).
- One condition is that minimum amounts of suffering should be caused (1). Human life is sacred as it was created by Allah, so it should not be threatened through fighting unless absolutely necessary (1).

Other valid answers will be accepted.

10   One mark will be awarded for providing each belief and a second mark for development of the belief up to a maximum of four marks. (4)
- Muslims believe that all life was created by Allah (1). The Qur'an details how Allah created the world and everything in it, including humans (1).
- Muslims believe that Allah created balance in the universe (1). Examples include night and day or the sea and the land (1).
- Muslims believe that it took long periods of time to create the universe (1). Islam teaches in the Qur'an that Allah intended to create the universe and did it over a long period of time, one part at a time (1).

Other valid answers will be accepted.

11   One mark will be awarded for providing a teaching and a second mark for development of the teaching up to a maximum of four marks. (4)

- Islam teaches that all human life is sacred, so euthanasia is wrong (1). Muslims are taught that as Allah created human life, only he can take it away (1).
- Islam teaches that suffering has a purpose and that euthanasia is wrong (1). The Qur'an teaches that only Allah has the right to decide when a person's life should end (Surah 3:145) (1).
- Islam teaches that there are alternatives to euthanasia (1). Hospices allow people to die with dignity so they do not need to end their lives through euthanasia (1).

Other valid answers will be accepted.

12   One mark will be awarded for providing each teaching and a second mark for development of the teaching up to a maximum of four marks. (4)
- The Qur'an teaches that Allah is compassionate and merciful (Surah 64:14) (1). Muslims believe that they should also develop these characteristics and forgive those who do wrong to them (1).
- Muhammad taught that if a person is sorry they should be forgiven (1). Muslims believe that Islam is a religion of peace and that they should try to put this into practice by being forgiving when someone is sorry (1).
- Muslims are taught to be forgiving towards others in order to be rewarded in the afterlife (1). Islam teaches that, on the Day of Judgement, they will be judged by Allah on how they have behaved and that forgiving others will help them to achieve paradise (1).

Other valid answers will be accepted.

13   One mark will be awarded for providing each belief and a second mark for development of the belief up to a maximum of four marks. (4)
- The use of weapons of mass destruction (WMD) is wrong as innocent life will be threatened (1). Muslims believe that Allah created all life, thereby making it sacred, so that to threaten or take it is wrong (1).
- The use of WMD is wrong as damage will be done to the environment (1). Islam teaches that the universe is Allah's creation and a gift to humanity so it should be protected (1).
- The use of WMD is wrong as these weapons do not fit Islamic rules about war (1). Islamic Just War theory says that too much damage would be caused by WMD for them to be justified (1).

Other valid answers will be accepted.

14   One mark will be awarded for providing each way and a second mark for development of the way up to a maximum of four marks. (4)
- Muslims may argue that science and Islam both help to explain how the universe was created (1). Muslims can accept the 'Big Bang' theory alongside their views about Allah creating the world (1).
- Muslims believe that Allah does not need a cause that explains his existence, as critics of the cosmological argument argue (1). Allah is divine, as his characteristics show, and it is not possible for Muslims to fully understand him (1).
- Muslims may argue that there must be a first cause of the universe and this cause must be Allah (1). They believe the teachings of the Qur'an that contain words from Allah supporting the cosmological argument (1).

Other valid answers will be accepted.

15   One mark will be awarded for providing each way and a second mark for development of the way up to a maximum of four marks. (4)
- Muslims may support Islamic charities that try to help those facing inequality (1). Examples of Islamic charities include Muslim Aid and Islamic Relief (1).
- Muslims may pray for those facing inequality (1). They believe Allah listens to their prayers and will support them in bringing about change (1).

- Muslims in positions of authority may speak out against inequality in the world (1). There are examples of imams educating others about inequality and working for change (1).

Other valid answers will be accepted.

134 (c) type questions

1 One mark will be awarded for providing each characteristic and a second mark for development of the characteristic up to a maximum of four marks. One further mark will be awarded for any relevant source of wisdom and authority. (5)
- One characteristic shown in the Qur'an is Allah's omnipotence (1). His great power can be seen through his creation of the universe (1): 'Blessed is He in whose hands is dominion, and He is over all things competent – [He] who created death and life to test you [as to] which of you is best in deed – and He is the Exalted in Might, the Forgiving – [And] who created seven heavens in layers …' (Surah 67:1–3) (1)
- One characteristic shown in the Qur'an is Allah's immanence (1). Muslims believe that Allah is close to and involved in the world, as shown through his use of prophets to communicate with humanity (1): 'Say, [O believers], "We have believed in Allah and what has been revealed to us and what has been revealed to Abraham and Ishmael and Isaac and Jacob …"' (Surah 2:136) (1)
- Tawhid is shown in the Qur'an (1). Muslims accept that there is only one God (1): 'Say, "He is Allah, [who is] One."' (Surah 112:1) (1)

Other valid answers will be accepted.

2 One mark will be awarded for providing each teaching and a second mark for development of the teaching up to a maximum of four marks. One further mark will be awarded for any relevant source of wisdom and authority. (5)
- Muslims are expected to marry (1). Islam teaches that the purpose of marriage is to bring a man and woman together to have children (1): 'Marry those among you who are single.' (Surah 24:32) (1)
- Marriage is intended to be for life (1). The nikkah – the contract made in marriage – is not intended to be broken and divorce is strongly disliked (1): 'The most hated of permissible things to Allah is divorce.' (Hadith) (1)
- Muslims believe that they will be rewarded for being married (1). Islam teaches that Muslim couples who marry and have children are contributing to the ummah and to Islam (1): 'When a husband and wife share intimacy, it is rewarded.' (Hadith) (1)

Other valid answers will be accepted.

3 One mark will be awarded for providing each way and a second mark for development of the way up to a maximum of four marks. One further mark will be awarded for any relevant source of wisdom and authority. (5)
- Some Muslims think that men and women have different and unequal roles (1). Men, as the protectors and providers, are understood to be in charge of women (1): 'Men are in charge of women by [right of] what Allah has given one over the other.' (Surah 4:34) (1)
- Some Muslims think that men and women have different but equal roles (1). Men and women's roles complement each other, with men providing for their family while women look after and care for the family (1): 'O Mankind! Be dutiful to your Lord, Who created you from a single person.' (Surah 4:1) (1)
- Some Muslims may see women as having the more important role in the Islamic family (1). Women raise the family and take care of the home, including the husband's property if he is absent (1): 'The righteous among the women of Quraish are those who are kind to their young ones and who look after their husband's property.' (Sahih al-Bukhari 64:278) (1)

Other valid answers will be accepted.

4 One mark will be awarded for providing each reason and a second mark for development of the reason up to a maximum of four marks. One further mark will be awarded for any relevant source of wisdom and authority. (5)
- Hajj is one of the Five Pillars of Islam (1). Muslims are expected to try to complete Hajj as it is a duty from Allah (1): 'The believing men and believing women are allies of one another. They enjoin what is right and forbid what is wrong and establish prayer and give zakah and obey Allah.' (Surah 9:71) (1)
- Hajj is seen to demonstrate equality between all Muslims (1). Muslims wear the same white clothing (ihram) and perform the same actions – for example, tawaf – to show that they are all the same (1): 'All people are equal like the teeth of a comb.' (Hadith) (1)
- Hajj demonstrates that all Muslims are part of the ummah (1.) This is the brotherhood of Muslims throughout the world and all are expected to complete Hajj (1): 'And proclaim to the people the Hajj.' (Surah 22:27) (1)

Other valid answers will be accepted.

5 One mark will be awarded for providing each response and a second mark for development of the response up to a maximum of four marks. One further mark will be awarded for any relevant source of wisdom and authority. (5)
- Some Muslims believe that other living things exist for the benefit of humans and so animals can be used for medical research (1). If it saves human life, experimentation is considered acceptable as human life was created by Allah to be special and to have dominion over the world (1): 'There is none amongst the Muslims who plants a tree or sows seeds, and then a bird, or a person or an animal eats from it, but is regarded as a charitable gift for him.' (Sahih al-Bukhari 3:513)
- Some Muslims may disagree with all animal experimentation arguing that animals are also Allah's creation and should therefore be respected (1). Muslims believe they have a duty of stewardship to care for animals and so they should not be used in experiments (1): 'Allah has appointed you his stewards over it.' (Hadith Bukhari) (1)
- Some Muslims may reject all animal experimentation because they believe they will be judged after death on how they have treated the world (1). As animals are Allah's creation, they have a right to be protected and not experimented on (1): 'And the earth He laid [out] for the creatures.' (Surah 55:10) (1)

Other valid answers will be accepted.

6 One mark will be awarded for providing each teaching and a second mark for development of the teaching up to a maximum of four marks. One further mark will be awarded for any relevant source of wisdom and authority. (5)
- Muslims believe that they should treat criminals fairly (1). The Qur'an teaches that prisoners should still be given human rights such as food, water and medical care (1): 'And they give food in spite of love for it to the needy, the orphan and the captive …' (Surah 76:8) (1)
- Muslims believe that criminals should have the right to a fair and just trial (1). Islam teaches that all people are created by Allah and therefore deserve fair treatment, including justice through fair punishment for criminals (1): 'O you who have believed, be persistently standing firm in justice …' (Surah 4:135) (1)
- Islam teaches that prisoners should not be tortured (1). Islam teaches that all humans are created by Allah and deserve respect as all life is sacred (1): 'O Mankind! Be dutiful to your Lord, Who created you from a single person.' (Surah 4:1) (1)

Other valid answers will be accepted.

7 One mark will be awarded for providing each teaching and a second mark for development of the teaching up to a maximum of four marks. One further mark will be awarded for any relevant source of wisdom and authority. (5)
- Islam teaches that war is allowed in certain circumstances (1). Islam teaches that it is acceptable to fight in order to defend

the religion of Islam (1): 'And what is [the matter] with you that you fight not in the cause of Allah.' (Surah 4:75) (1)

- Muslims believe peace is important and that Muslims should work for peace, not war, in the world (1). As Allah is merciful and peaceful, all methods of peacefully resolving conflict should be tried before turning to war (1): 'And the servants of the Most Merciful are those who walk upon the earth easily, and when the ignorant address them [harshly] they say [words of] peace.' (Surah 25:63) (1)
- Muslims believe Allah is merciful and forgiving and that they should follow his example in times of conflict (1). Islam teaches that Muslims should avoid conflict and fight only in certain circumstances, such as to protect the innocent from harm or in self-defence (1): 'Fight in the way of Allah those who fight you.' (Surah 2:190) (1)

Other valid answers will be accepted.

8 One mark will be awarded for providing each way and a second mark for development of the way up to a maximum of four marks. One further mark will be awarded for any relevant source of wisdom and authority. (5)

- All Muslims attach some importance to religious experience as Muhammad himself underwent a religious experience (1) when the Qur'an was revealed to him (1): 'It is not but a revelation revealed. Taught to him by one intense in strength.' (Surah 53:4–5) (1)
- Some Muslims believe other forms of revelation are more important than religious experience (1). For example, some Muslims place greater importance on the Qur'an and the prophets as sources of authority than on religious experience (1): 'We have believed in Allah and what has been revealed to us and what has been revealed to Abraham and Ishmael and Isaac and Jacob …' (Surah 2:136) (1)
- Some Muslims, such as Sufis, are more mystical and place great importance on religious experience (1). They may even try to induce experiences as they feel these allow a personal connection to Allah (1): 'Those who do not know say, "Why does Allah not speak to us or there come to us a sign?" ' (Surah 2:118) (1)

Other valid answers will be accepted.

9 One mark will be awarded for providing each teaching and a second mark for development of the teaching up to a maximum of four marks. One further mark will be awarded for any relevant source of wisdom and authority. (5)

- Religious freedom is important because it is a human right (1). Some Muslims believe that all religions should be respected because Islam recognises the truths of other faiths such as Christianity and Judaism (1): 'And Allah is hearing and knowing. Allah is the ally of those who believe.' (Surah 2:256–257) (1)
- Some Muslims may recognise that while all religions contain parts of the truth, only Islam contains the whole truth (1). They may believe that other faiths became corrupted and that Islam is the only way to understand Allah better (1): 'Say, "O People of the Scripture, come to a word that is equitable between us and you." But if they turn away, then say, "Bear witness that we are Muslims [submitting to Him]." ' (Surah 3:64) (1)
- Some Muslims believe that it does not matter which religion a person belongs to (1). They accept that all righteous people will be favoured by Allah and therefore respect all religions (1): 'So whoever disbelieves in Taghut and believes in Allah has grasped the most trustworthy handhold with no break in it. And Allah is Hearing and Knowing.' (Surah 2:256) (1)

Other valid answers will be accepted.

135 (d) type questions

1 "All Muslims should get married." Be sure to make your points specific, and refer to teachings and views, as you are instructed. You can support your arguments with Qur'an or other teachings. Make sure you give balanced views and then draw a conclusion – make sure you say why this is your conclusion. (12)

Arguments for the statement:

- Islam teaches that all Muslims should get married as this is what Allah intended. The Qur'an teaches: 'Marry those among you who are single' (Surah 24:32). Marriage was given by Allah as a gift for a man and woman in which they can join together and have children.
- Marriage is important to Muslims as it is believed to bring stability to society. Muslims believe the family unit, in which the couple are married, provides the ideal environment for raising good Muslim children within the Islamic faith.
- Islamic teachings do not support ideas of cohabitation as they hold traditional views about marriage. They believe that sexual relationships prior to marriage are wrong and Muslims often enter into arranged marriages to ensure a good match.

Arguments against the statement:

- Non-religious people may believe that marriage is no longer necessary in today's society. They accept that couples may wish to cohabit in order to get to know each other prior to considering marriage.
- Non-religious people may hold different views to Muslims about the purpose of marriage, believing that some couples may not wish to have children and therefore may not want to get married.
- Some Muslims may not want to get married. They may instead choose to dedicate their lives to Allah in another way.

Other valid answers will be accepted.

2 "Greater jihad is more important than lesser jihad." Be sure to make your points specific, and refer to teachings and views, as you are instructed. You can support your arguments with Qur'anic or other teachings. Make sure you give balanced views and then draw a conclusion – make sure you say why this is your conclusion. In this question, three of the marks awarded will be for your spelling, punctuation and grammar, and your use of specialist terminology. (15)

Arguments for the statement:

- Many Muslims will agree with the statement as greater jihad is emphasised more in the Qur'an, thus making it more important. This view is supported by Muhammad, who said: 'The person who struggles so that Allah's word is supreme is the one serving Allah's cause.'
- Greater jihad is an inner struggle in which Muslims strive to resist temptation and evil. Muslims would argue that overcoming temptation and evil on a daily basis and staying focused on the duties a Muslim has to perform is far harder than lesser jihad, therefore making it more important.
- Many Muslims understand greater jihad to be the true meaning of jihad itself, so giving it more importance. Greater jihad is a personal battle rather than a religious battle.

Arguments against the statement:

- Some Muslims may disagree with the statement, as lesser jihad is important when the religion of Islam as a whole is attacked. They may feel that defending Islam against global attack is more important than any personal battle.
- There may be times when lesser jihad becomes more important than greater jihad, so the statement may only be relevant at certain times. For example, if the religion of Islam is attacked, this becomes the most important thing.
- Because there are set criteria that must be followed, some Muslims may argue that lesser jihad is more important. Lesser jihad can only be declared by the right authority, if it is the last resort and for the purpose of defending Islam.

Other valid answers will be accepted.

3 "It is never right to fight." Be sure to make your points specific, and refer to teachings and views, as you are instructed. You can support your arguments with Qur'anic or other teachings. Make sure you give balanced views and

then draw a conclusion – make sure you say why this is your conclusion. (12)

Arguments for the statement:

- Islam is a religion of peace, so this should always be the focus. There are many examples of how important peace is in Islam, including the way that Muslims greet each other with signs of peace. This shows that Muslims' first thoughts are always for peace and not conflict.
- Islam teaches that Allah created the world with the intention that peace would be part of his creation. Muslims place more emphasis on greater jihad – the personal daily struggle – than on lesser jihad – war.
- Muslims believe that the ummah demonstrates ideas of peace and that when there is conflict, the Muslim community should find peaceful methods to resolve it. The Qur'an advocates pacifism or passive resistance and does not support fighting (Surah 5:28).

Arguments against the statement:

- Some Muslims believe that war is sometimes necessary in order to bring about peace and that, therefore, fighting is justified in certain circumstances. One reason that they would accept is to defend the religion of Islam from attack.
- Some Muslims follow teachings in the Qur'an that support fighting. Islam is not a pacifist religion and some passages suggest that it is acceptable to fight and kill an enemy when necessary (Surah 9:5).
- Non-religious people may believe that fighting threatens life and is never right. They may feel that life is too valuable to be put at risk and that only peaceful methods should be used to resolve conflict.

Other valid answers will be accepted.

"It is wrong for Muslims to be wealthy." Be sure to make your points specific, and refer to teachings and views, as you are instructed. You can support your arguments with Qur'anic or other teachings. Make sure you give balanced views and then draw a conclusion – make sure you say why this is your conclusion. (12)

Arguments for the statement:

- Islam has many teachings on how Muslims should work to help others and act against social injustice. The Qur'an teaches that Muslims should be 'regular in charity' (Surah 2:110), and Muslims believe it is important to follow these teachings and to use their wealth for good purposes.
- Many Muslims would agree that Islam teaches the idea of sharing and caring for the poor. One of the Five Pillars of Islam is Zakah, which encourages Muslims to share their wealth with those in need.
- Muslims believe that it is important to be good khalifahs or stewards. They believe everything in the universe was created by Allah – including humans – and that they have a responsibility to use their money to help bring about greater equality.

Arguments against the statement:

- Some Muslims believe that wealth is a gift from Allah. Although it is not wrong for a Muslim to be wealthy, many Muslims often choose to give sadaqah – voluntary charitable donations – to use their money to help others where possible.
- Islam teaches that the more a person has, the more good they can do. Muslims believe they will be judged by Allah after death on the way they behaved and acted, which also includes whether they used their money wisely.
- Muslims understand that although it is not wrong for a Muslim to be wealthy, money is not the most important thing in life and it is more important to strive to live their lives as Allah intended.

Other valid answers will be accepted.

Notes